D1593395

We Are A Part Of History:
THE STORY OF THE ORPHAN TRAINS

"Street Arabs," New York, ca. mid-19th century. *(Courtesy Jacob Riis Collection, New York.)*

We Are A Part Of History:
The Story Of The
Orphan Trains

by Michael Patrick,
Evelyn Sheets and Evelyn Trickel

The Donning Company/Publishers
184 Business Park Drive, Suite 106 Virginia Beach, VA 23462

First Printing 1990 by:
The Lightning Tree, Santa Fe, New Mexico

Second Printing with index 1994 by:
The Donning Company/Publishers
184 Business Park Drive, Suite 106
Virginia Beach, VA 23462

   Nancy Schneiderheinze, Reprint Project Director
   Mary Elizabeth Downing, Reprint Research Coordinator

Library of Congress Cataloging in Publication Data:
Patrick, Michael, 1935—
     We are a part of history: the story of the orphan trains / by Michael
Patrick, Evelyn Sheets, and Evelyn Trickel.
        p.   cm.
     Includes bibliographical references and index
     ISBN: 0-89865-921-3
     1. Orphans—New York (N.Y.)—Biography 2. Abandoned children—New
York (N.Y.)—Biography 3. Adoptees—Missouri—Biography.
I. Sheets, Evelyn, 1919-1989. II. Trickel, Evelyn, 1932- . III. Title. IV. Title:
Orphan trains.
     HV986.P38 1990
     362.7'34'092273—dc20
     [B]   90-6190
                                                                          CIP

Printed in the United States of America

Michael Patrick and Evelyn Trickel
dedicate this book
to the memory of Evelyn Sheets
1919-1989

Contents

List of Illustrations

Preface and Acknowledgments

ONE AFTERNOON in 1980, when I was president of the Missouri Folklore Society, I had a telephone call from a lady who identified herself as Evelyn Sheets. Although Mrs. Sheets, who lived in Trenton, Missouri, was not a member of the Society, she was planning to drive 285 miles from Trenton to Rolla to find out just what folklorists did. Her interest had been aroused by a newspaper announcement of the annual meeting.

Mrs. Sheets did not have an extensive background in higher education, but she had great curiosity and a thirst for knowledge of all kinds. In Trenton, while her husband had been manager of Mattingly's five-and-dime, she had taken classes at the junior college and with the University of Missouri. She became an adjunct instructor in adult education, teaching genealogy. At the same time she was employed full time as a city clerk.

After her trip to Rolla, her interest in folklore increased. She began teaching an adult class in folklore at the junior college and doing research.

As her first research project, she went about the cemeteries of the area, capturing local history from tombstones and epitaphs. The result was "Grundy County History in Stone," a slide presentation shown throughout the state as a model history/folklore demonstration. Her personal friendship with most of the people in the county enabled her to augment her findings with many interviews.

Her next project, "A Place Called Poosey," detailed the history of Grundy County through interviews and early records. The area was known as Poosey because the first settlers named it after the Po Indians of Kentucky, their home state.

For this project she was joined by a friend and former student, Evelyn Trickel. The two women had met forty years earlier, when Mrs. Trickel as a teenager went to work at Mattingly's. They were fast friends from that time on. At the time of their first research together, Evelyn Trickel had for seven years been director of the Adult Basic Education Program at Trenton Junior College. She also taught accounting, economics, general business courses and folk literature for adults. She is now the area sales representative for Metropolitan Life Insurance and a certifed National Association Life Underwriter. But she still teaches a course each semester at the junior college.

Because of their projects together, the two women became known among research people throughout Missouri as "The Evelyns."

Their work on Poosey was followed by "Up and Down Bound in Missouri River Steamboats, 1819-1900," presented at the Missouri Folklore Society in 1984. This project led them to focus on the Saluda steamboat explosion which occurred on Good Friday, 1852, in Lexington, Missouri.

Then one day while teaching an adult class in genealogy, Evelyn Sheets was asked by one of the women in the class if it would be possible to trace the ancestry of someone who had come to the Midwest as one of a trainload of homeless children shipped out from the slums of New York City. Never daunted by any challenge, Mrs. Sheets set out to see if this was possible. She discovered that it was.

She also discovered that at the time those "orphan trains" were running, Trenton was a division point on the Rock Island Railroad, and many of those who had ridden the trains were still living in the area. She immediately started seeking out those people or their descendants and acquaintances. And thus, with the help of Evelyn Trickel, the orphan train project was launched.

Over the years I had kept in touch with Evelyn Sheets by telephone and through her presentations at meetings of the Missouri Folklore Society and the Missouri Gerontology Institute. In the winter of 1984 I received a call from her, asking if I would serve as consultant on a grant from the Missouri Humanities Council, supporting research on the orphan trains. At first I tried to plead that my own research and my teaching kept me too busy to be involved in anything else.

Her response was emphatic: "This is important. You need to do this." Convinced by her tone, I agreed.

With a small grant from the Humanities Council, The Evelyns set to work. They traveled and talked, collected photographs, wrote a script and prepared a slide presentation. They also planned a reunion of surviving orphans, to be held in Trenton on Labor Day weekend, 1985.

In the meantime, some 285 miles away, I gave advice by phone and mail, edited their script, and found my interest in the project increasing day by day. But it was on Labor Day, at that first reunion in Trenton, that the orphan trains truly came alive for me, as I talked with actual riders of those trains and with their children and grandchildren. Meeting these men and women who had endured so much emotional and physical hardship, and survived, was a lesson in the indomitability of the human spirit. They seemed to have learned at an early age to live courageously, without complaint. As Rose Cranor, one of the train riders, said to me, "You have to deal with life as you find it."

Rose Cranor had come to the reunion despite a recent heart attack. She was a delight, with a wealth of information. When she died, three weeks later, before I could talk with her again, I felt I had lost a friend.

There were three other orphan train riders at that reunion, Lester Studer and the brothers Arthur and Noah Lawyer. Another rider, Gus Jahne, had planned to attend but died a few weeks before. His son did attend the reunion, along with twenty-four other descendants of the orphans. Talking with those good people, I realized more vividly than ever the impact their lives have had on succeeding generations and will continue to have.

It was that day at the reunion that Evelyn Sheets announced to me, "Evelyn and I have decided that this project deserves a book. And we want you to write it."

With the enthusiasm of The Evelyns and those first encounters with the orphan train riders, I became totally involved in the project. For the last five years I have done little else in my free time. The three of us traveled the Midwest doing interviews, written hundreds of letters and received hundreds from people wanting to provide information. We have talked for hours by telephone to the riders and relatives.

In New York City I met with people at the Children's Aid Society and the New York Foundling Hospital, who graciously helped me with research into public records and published materials. When no money was available from grants, all of us without hesitation spent our own money for travel, phone calls and other related expenses. The Evelyns and I worked closely together, the project being a collaboration in every sense of the word.

Our work was progressing well when in 1986 a catastrophe occurred which affected not only the research but our lives as well. Evelyn Sheets was a woman of such energy, of such an active mind, that she usually had several projects going at once. One of these was to find and interview people who had seen Halley's Comet in 1910. Quite early on the morning of March 21 she and a group of friends drove out to the intersection of Missouri highways 8 and 148, where they might have a good view of the comet. Mrs. Sheets parked her car on the north side of the intersection and walked across the road to the south side. Later, as she was returning, she was struck by another car. In addition to multiple fractures, she suffered massive head injuries. She did not recover. After lying in a coma for over three years, Evelyn Sheets died on June 16, 1989.

In the years since the accident occurred, Evelyn Trickel and I have gone on with the project. But we sorely miss Evelyn Sheets, her energy and enthusiasm for the work. We miss her as a friend.

As news of our work spread, we were greatly pleased to learn that many who had not known of the orphan trains before had become interested. For example, Mary Ellen Johnson of Springdale, Arkansas, became so interested that she organized the Orphan Train Heritage Society, dedicated to the locating, documenting and preservation of information about the riders. The Society keeps a register of the orphans and their descendants, maintains a library, publishes a quarterly newsletter and holds an annual reunion in Springdale. They also present two awards for outstanding effort in expanding and preserving the history of the orphan trains: the Brace Award, honoring the memory of Charles Loring Brace, first director of the New York Children's Aid Society and instigator of the Society's orphan train program; and the Sister Irene Award, in memory of the woman who directed the placement policy of the New York Foundling Hospital.

Interest in the trains has also resulted in a play. Written by Jay Turley, it is called simply "Orphan Trains" and is performed by local groups, under his direction, in a number of Missouri towns. Jay Turley first heard of our research in 1987 at the Governor's Conference on Aging and immediately got in touch. We talked together for two hours and I provided him with material we had written. He was so moved by the story that he spent the entire night writing the play, finishing just at daybreak. It has become his most popular work.

Throughout our work we have received invaluable assistance, support, and encouragement from many individuals and organizations, to all of whom we wish to express our appreciation: To the English Department and the College of Arts and Sciences at the University of Missouri-Rolla; to the Missouri Humanities Council and the Missouri Gerontological Institute for grants which helped support our research; to the staffs of the Jewett Norris Library of Grundy County, the Western Historical Manuscript Collection, the library of the University of Missouri-Columbia, and the inter-library loan department of the University of Missouri-Rolla.

We are indebted also to Barbara Ternes and Ethel Lambert of the New York Children's Aid Society and the Sisters of the New York Foundling Hospital; to Eloise Thomsen of Omaha, creator of the Orphan Register; to Dr. Phil Leighly, professor of Metallurgical Engineering at the University of Missouri-Rolla, for materials on the British transportation of children (researched while on sabbatical leave in England); and to all those who wrote and broadcast stories which helped us generate interest in our project, as well as locate orphan train riders or their descendants. Special mention should be made of Brian Burns and Pat Sullivan of the Kansas City *Star* and Eric Johnson, writing for *The Junior Scholastic*. And our sincere thanks to Linda Brammel, who has typed and retyped with patience.

For background information we have drawn on previously published materials, principally Charles Loring Brace's autobiography, *The Dangerous Classes of New York and Twenty Years Work Among Them,* first published in 1880 and reprinted in 1967; also from *Orphan Train: A Novel,* by James Magnuson and Dorothea Petrie, 1978; *Children West: A History of the Placing-Out System of the New York Children's Aid Society, 1853-1890,* by Miriam Z. Langsam, 1964; and *Searching for Home: Three Families from the Orphan Trains,* by Martha Nelson Vogt and Christina Vogt. Published in 1985, this book is a vivid account of the trains from the perspective of three families in Michigan.

All material previously unpublished is drawn from personal interviews which Evelyn Sheets, Evelyn Trickel and I conducted; from letters and documents supplied by surviving riders of the orphan trains or their descendants, and from one foster parent, Mrs. Sadie Dickman Urton, who at the time we met her was about to celebrate her one-hundredth birthday. It is these men and women to whom we are most indebted. We know that Evelyn Sheets would want them to receive her deepest gratitude. On her behalf, and ours, we thank them all.

MICHAEL PATRICK
University of Missouri-Rolla
July 1989

We Are A Part Of History:
THE STORY OF THE
ORPHAN TRAINS

1: Street Arabs

A very small boy stood upon a heap of gravel for the honor of Rum Alley. He was throwing stones and howling urchins from Devil's Row were circling madly about the head and pelting him.

So begins Stephen Crane's novel, *Maggie, Girl of the Streets*. Further down, in the second chapter,

. . .they entered into a dark region where, from a careening building, a dozen gruesome doorways gave up loads of babies to the street and the gutter. A wind of early autumn raised yellow dust from the cobbles and swirled it against an hundred windows. Long streamers of garments fluttered from fire escapes. In all unhandy places there were buckets, brooms, rags, and bottles. In the streets infants played or fought with other infants in the way of vehicles.

The story, which appeared in 1893, shocked the sensibilities of its readers. Because of its harsh reality, his depiction of the slums of New York City and children on the street, no publisher would accept it. When it did appear, printed at the author's own expense, many booksellers refused to sell it. And many of those who bought it criticized it as emphasizing only the negative side of urban life.

Crane's description was accurate. But the book might have been rejected altogether had he described conditions in the slums as New York social workers saw them.

Raw sewage floated in the gutters. Because of the lack of sanitation and bathing facilities the odors of filth permeated the tenements and overflowed into the streets. Garbage was strewn everywhere. The streets were scenes of human refuse and dereliction of all kinds. Men crippled from industrial accidents or too old to work survived by begging, petty thievery or as best they could. Others, destroyed by alcohol or drugs, lay in the gutters or wandered the sidewalks preying on the weak.

Women carrying venereal diseases sold themselves openly, day and night. Day and night, thieves, thugs, and sadists roamed the dark alleys, seeking whatever pleasure and profit they could find. A descent into New York's Lower East Side was as horrifying as Dante's descent into the Inferno. Indeed, the area became known as Hell's Kitchen. The situation was so hopeless and involved so many children that social workers and reformers saw no solution to the problem.

The problem of the slums was a product of American immigration policies of the nineteenth and early twentieth centuries. Through the nineteenth century there were three distinct stages of immigration noted by most historians. The first, usually called Celtic, lasted about thirty years, from 1830-1860. Though many immigrants of that period came from the Upper Rhine Valley and adjacent districts of Germany, the majority came from Ireland, the Scottish Highlands and Wales. During the second stage, 1860-1890, immigrants were predominantly English. But the largest Scandinavian immigration also took place during those years, while migration from Germany and Austria continued. In the third stage, from 1890-1914, the predominant groups were Slavs and Mediterranean. These three stages involved an estimated thirty-five million people.

Part of the impetus for this mass movement was the attraction of cheap land in the United States. In some parts of the West the federal government had granted the railroads fifty and even one hundred mile right-of-ways to encourage development of the unsettled areas. The railroads in turn sold off this land at low cost to speculators, religious groups, town planners and immigration societies. In Europe these immigration societies published advertisements and pamphlets describing the utopian aspects of America and drawings of bucolic scenes and town sites surveyed along the railroad right-of-way. The railroads further promoted the movement by organizing emigrant trains as the least expensive way to transport large numbers of new settlers. Far from being standard passenger trains, uncomfortable as they must have been in that period, these emigrant trains were merely boxcars fitted with wooden benches.

Ethnic newspapers published in the United States also encouraged emigration. In her story, *Neighbor Rosicky*, Willa Cather tells how a Czech immigrant, working as a tailor in New York City, became a Nebraska farmer. "He began to think seriously about the articles he had read in the Bohemian papers, describing prosperous Czech farming communities in the West. He subscribed for a Bohemian paper printed in Chicago, then one printed in Omaha. His mind got farther and farther west."

Today, throughout the West and Midwest, dozens upon dozens of communities and rural areas reflect this immigration pattern. For example, towns such as Millstadt and Belleville in Illinois and areas such as the Missouri River Valley from Augusta to Rhineland and Hermann still retain their German flavor. Rosati, Missouri, a hamlet near St. James, on what is now the Burlington-Northern Railroad, still has a strong Italian element. According to local folklore, the town was founded when a group of Italian immigrants traveling on the Frisco railroad were dropped off in the middle of the prairie and told this was the land they had bought. Never daunted, they began to farm, planted orchards and vineyards, and, as Robert Ramsey tells us in *Our Storehouse of Missouri Place Names,* named the place after Joseph Rosati, the second Catholic bishop of St. Louis. Today, though the population has dwindled to about fifty townspeople, there are numerous grape growers and three wineries in the surrounding area, as well as a restaurant with the good Italian name of Cardetti's. As late as 1960 Phelps County supervisors of the presidential election were said to have had a difficult time finding judges for the Rosati polling places who spoke English.

But while many immigrants did settle in rural areas, many more did not. The land was not always available to them, or they lacked the specialized, practical skills to become homesteaders. With the industrial expansion in America the European immigrants, for the most part, settled in cities where they attempted to preserve their ethnicity, at the same time providing an abundant source of cheap labor.

This phenomenal urban growth made the cities collections of ethnic neighborhoods. In New York City, as early as 1830, the section known as Five Points had become predominantly Irish. By the next generation the Irish area covered most of the Lower East Side. By 1850, just north of the Irish district, was the German area known as Kleindeutchland, extending from the Bowery to the tenth, eleventh and thirteenth wards. Soon on the Lower East Side the Italians established Little Italy.

Because New York was the port of entry for the three great waves of nineteenth century immigration it was formed, culturally and geographically, by its ethnicity. It became a city of slums. Toward the end of the century the tenements housed more than 1,200,000 of the poor. When these buildings became too crowded to hold more, thousands were forced to live in the streets, under bridges, under steps or in open lots.

In 1846 the New York almshouse commissioner described the situation to the Common Council of the city in desperate terms. When the immigrants came to America, he wrote, "surrounded by their young and innocent offspring, little did they imagine the trials to which they would be exposed, but at length they discover to their sorrow, and very natural discontent, that the foul steerage of some ocean-tossed ship is to form the filthy receptacle of their persons."[1]

Then upon arriving in the United States with great expectations of land, opportunity, and wealth, their hopes were totally destroyed by the bureaucracy of the immigration service, the arbitrary enforcement of the rules of entry, and the utter confusion caused by new customs and language. The commissioner described their arrival in vivid terms.

> Large numbers of these unfortunate emigrants, as soon as they quit the decks of vessels, having no home to which to direct their movements, wander through the streets in a state of utter desolation, until some benevolent hand, appalled by the misery and wretchedness before him, guides their prostrated frames and tottering gait to the Park almshouse board; and here is exhibited so sickening a picture of human destitution and suffering as no pen, however eloquent in the sad gloom of misfortune's description, could well paint the illustration of the dark and solemn truth. The deplorable infirmity of their desolate unhappiness must be *seen and felt* to

be appreciated, and then, too often find amid the motley groups some with the last gasp of expiration issuing from their cold and blanched lips, forms a scene of dismay and distress too agonizing to look upon with any other than feelings of horror and overwhelming sympathy.[2]

The commissioner's language is rather overblown in the nineteenth century style, but it should be remembered that because of the genteel tradition he had to avoid mentioning many vices, diseases, crimes, and deprivations, using instead the euphemistic rhetoric of charity workers.

Even for those immigrants who did succeed in finding work and living space, their lot was hard. Without the protection of government agencies and labor unions, industrial laborers faced permanent injuries that would prevent them from working. They were also vulnerable to frequent lay-offs due to the economy. Because there were many more workers available than there were jobs, a competitive market could reduce wages to below living standards.

In some cases the younger members could add to the family's income by selling newspapers, shining shoes or selling matches on street corners. But often even those families who had achieved a precarious foothold found that they could not support their young. It was the children, then, who became the system's most tragic victims.

A few early charitable institutions had taken in abandoned children, one of the first being Bellevue Hospital, founded in 1736 as part of the New York City Almshouse. Unfortunately, most of the children were then sent to Riker's Island Infant Hospital, where, according to one source, over ninety percent of them died.[3]

Those who did not wind up on Riker's Island fared very little better. During the periods of the great migrations city streets were filled with abandoned children running about unsupervised and uncared for. These were the urchins whom the police dubbed "street arabs." Some of them had simply been turned out by their hard-pressed parents. Others had left home voluntarily, escaping the squalor and abuse of the tenements. They existed by any means at hand, by begging, picking pockets, snatching purses and by shoplifting. Some ran errands for gambling operations. Some were forced into

Around the middle of the 19th century, some 30,000 abandoned children lived in New York streets. *(Courtesy Jacob Riis Collection, New York.)*

prostitution. Their lives were generally a steady progression from petty offenses to serious crime to imprisonment. Cast out, unwanted, fighting to survive, these small street arabs were considered "dangerous classes," a threat to society.

Into this desperate situation stepped a pioneering social worker, the Reverend Charles Loring Brace. Although he was educated for the clergy and ordained as a Congregational minister, Brace at twenty-six felt that he was unsuited for the pulpit. In 1853 he, along with a few other reformers in New York City, founded the Children's Aid Society. Unlike earlier orphan asylums and almshouses, the Society sought to do more than provide food, lodging and clothing. Their goal was to offer the children educational and trade opportunities.

One of the first moves was the establishment of industrial schools. With his great American belief in the saving grace of education and work, Brace rather naïvely believed that this would promptly turn the street arabs into useful members of society. Although in some instances these schools were successful, attendance was usually sporadic, with only a limited number of children learning a useful trade.

Brace also believed that Sabbath day lectures would change the course of young lives. But personal experience soon showed him that such lectures had little effect upon the arabs. When and if they did come to the Sunday School lessons, they were rowdy, profane and irreverent. Even so, Brace could describe these "Boys' Meetings" with good humor. "Sometimes the salutatory exercises from the street were showers of stones; sometimes a general scrimmage occurred over the benches; again the visitors or missionaries were pelted by some opposition gang, or bitter enemies of the lads who attended the meeting."[4]

Although not many of these children fit the mold of Horatio Alger's heroes, Brace had an understanding of and affection for them, especially the newsboys. He saw in them a love of life and a sense of humor that made them well worth saving from the hardships of the street. To him their ebullience at the meetings only reflected their energy and quick wit.

He seems to have enjoyed their replies to missionaries who in the course of a sermon tried to question the boys. For instance, a minister once asked them, "In this parable, my dear boys, of Pharisee and the publican, what is meant by the 'publican'?" Came the answer, "Alderman, sire, wot keeps a pot house!"

Asked about "the great end of man,"—"When is he happiest? How would you feel happiest?"—the boys replied, "When we'd plenty of hard cash, sir!"

Still another missionary said to them, "My dear boys, when your father and mother forsake you, who will take you up?" Their reply was serious and realistic, "The purlice, sir, the purlice."

Although Brace understood such forthright response to superficial or hypocritical speakers, he realized that "ungoverned, prematurely sharp, and accustomed to all vileness, as these lads were, words which came forth from the depths of a man's or woman's heart would always touch some hidden chord."[5] And though he felt that homeless boys had rather a good time of it, wandering the streets, living by their wits, free from adult supervision, he also felt that they needed to get off the street and into homes.

One of the early efforts of the Children's Aid Society was to establish lodging houses for newsboys. At first, these were regarded by the boys "with some suspicion and much contempt." They thought the lodging houses were an attempt to make them go to Sunday School, and they suspected the superintendent, C. C. Tracy, of being a street preacher. Actually, he was a carpenter. Though the boys planned at first to disrupt the lodgings, they quickly realized that a good bed for six cents and a supper for four cents were worth some religious prodding..

Sunday School was introduced in what Brace considered a "discreet manner." After the boys had been impressed by a public funeral, Superintendent Tracy suggested that they listen to him read from the Bible. Soon they were discussing the miraculous stories and relating to Christ as one of the homeless, like themselves. Perhaps hymn singing gave them more religious instruction than anything else; they entered into it with gusto, singing those hymns that seemed very personal to them, such as "There's a Rest for the Weary" and "There's a Light in the Window."

After the lodging houses, the next step by the Children's Aid Society was to get the boys educated in some manner and put them to work. To allow the boys to work during the day and avoid conflict with public schools (even though children generally ignored them) they started an evening school.

Ever men of the nineteenth century, Brace and his associates in the Society believed that the strongest moral and spiritual lessons derived from capitalism. To instill in the boys the value of work and earning—and to overcome their faith in gambling—the lodging house established a savings bank for the boys and paid a rather high rate of interest. In Brace's estimation, this gave them ". . .the 'sense of property,' and the desire for accumulation, which economists tell us, is the basis of all civilization."[6] But there was a folktale among the newsboys about a news seller who had become rich by gambling on policy tickets. And Brace had to admit that moral instruction in capitalism never completely ended gambling. The boys continued to buy policy tickets.

The street girls presented entirely different problems, especially when they were involved in prostitution. The Reverend Brace's attitudes reflect the prejudices of the day. As girls were considered purer than boys, they were therefore degraded by sexual experiences, as the boys were not. While the boys might survive the streets with their personalities intact, girls were psychologically destroyed. Brace's efforts on their behalf were well-meaning but naïve.

The Rev. Charles Loring Brace.

He felt their problems could be solved by industrial schools. It was his belief that many of the girls were ashamed to go to public schools because of their ragged clothes. Therefore, to overcome their vices all they needed was exposure to the dignity, dress and morality of upperclass ladies who were their teachers.

Of these volunteer, well-to-do teachers Brace wrote, "As these ladies, many of them of remarkable character and culture, began to show the fruits of civilization to these poor little barbarians, the thought seemed to strike me—though hardly capable of being expressed—that here was a goodness and piety they had never known or conceived."[7]

Throughout his published works Brace's optimism never diminishes. But optimism was not enough to solve the complicated problems of the street arabs. There were so many of them: children without parents; those with at least one living parent—a widow, an abandoned wife or father—unable to support the young; the younger children of large families, placed in orphanages, leaving older brothers and sisters behind. There were the abandoned, illegitimate waifs, and newborn babies left on doorsteps, in rainbarrels or on the sidewalks. At one time an estimated 30,000 homeless children filled the streets of the New York slums. Orphanages, lodging houses and foster homes could not be found or built to hold them all.

One year after the establishment of the Children's Aid

Society the Reverend Brace recognized that some radical plan must be developed to alleviate such conditions. With his usual energetic optimism and initiative he found one.

Notes to Chapter 1

1. Edith Abbott, *Immigration: Select Documents and Case Records* (New York: Ayers Co., 1969), p. 28.

2. Abbott, p. 27.

3. Mabel Potter Daggett, "The Child Without a Home," *Delineator* (October 1907), p. 510.

4. Charles Loring Brace, *The Dangerous Classes of New York and Twenty Years Work Among Them* (reprint, Montclair, N. J.: Patterson Smith, 1967), p. 80.

5. Brace, pp. 80-81.

6. Brace, pp. 104-105.

7. Brace, p. 139.

2: Brace's Solution

THE PROPOSAL WHICH the Reverend Brace made to the Children's Aid Society was not original. Such a plan had been in effect in Boston as early as 1849. Brace simply borrowed it. Although he was to add his own touch to it, the plan basically was that of sending orphan children from eastern city slums to foster homes in other parts of the country.

Transporting children from one geographic area to another was not new to the nineteenth century. It had been practiced in ancient Jewish and early Christian cultures. In England it had been a common feature of the indenture system, whereby orphans, often very young, were sent out as servants or apprentices. For example, when the Mayflower sailed to America in 1620, four orphans named More were aboard. Of these only one survived the first winter in Plymouth Colony. (It may be noted here that transportation continued well into the twentieth century. From 1867 to 1914 English children were removed to Canada. During World War II both Canada and the United States provided temporary refuge for children from war-torn Britain. Following the war, thousands were sent to Australia.)

The Boston emigration system was the first to be established in this country. "Although precise details are lacking, by 1850 Children's Mission orphan trains were used to place children on farms throughout New England. Until this practice was interrupted by the Civil War, agents took bands of thirty to fifty children by train to New England and Middle Western communities where local churches made informal indenture, apprenticeship, foster care, or adoption arrangements in respectable families."[1] One of the men involved with this program was J. E. Williams, a Boston banker, who later became a founding member of the Children's Aid Society and its longtime secretary. From him Brace learned of the program, took up the idea, and went to work.

One change he was to make involved the matter of indenture. The Boston Children's Mission allowed the children they sent out to become indentured servants, either as farm or household workers. Brace found this aspect of the plan unacceptable and decided that orphans from the Children's Aid Society were not to be indentured. While the children were expected to work in exchange for room, board and education, the Society rejected the contractual basis of the indenture and apprenticeship systems and maintained legal control of the children. As Miriam Z. Langsam writes in her study of the Society's placing-out system, "the Society or the parents retained legal guardianship and never surrendered it to the employer unless he wanted to adopt the child. This in Brace's eyes averted some of the problems of the indenture system, at least in theory." She goes on to say, "On the other hand, it also allowed irresponsible or greedy farmers to throw out boys after a season of work in order to escape the necessity of feeding them during the winter months. The child, however, could always appeal to the Society or the courts for help."[2]

In rejecting indentured servitude, Brace was emphasizing what he called "the family plan," whereby children would be taken into homes and made part of the family, provided for as for natural children with all the rights and responsibilities. The family plan, he argued, would not only be the least expensive way of solving juvenile delinquency, begging and street crime, but would greatly benefit the children. Using statistics from the Massachusetts Board of State Charities, he showed that mortality in the orphan asylums could be reduced from thirty to forty percent to "twenty to thirty-five per cent in good single families, the last being scarcely above the normal death-rate of all infants." It would also, he maintained, be less expensive than building more orphan homes in the city, as others wanted to do.

Why will our benevolent ladies and gentlemen keep up the old monastic ideas of the necessity of herding these unfortunate children in one building? Here there are thousands of homes awaiting the foundlings, without money and without price, where the child would have the best advantages the country could afford.[3]

Orphan homes were filled to capacity. *(Courtesy Jacob Riis Collection, New York.)*

Equally important was his conviction that rural areas offered the greatest benefit to these children of the slums. The best homes, he felt, were to be found in the rural Midwest (which he referred to as the West). In such environs the children would have the idyllic existence denied them on the city streets.

> In every American community, especially in a western one, there are many spare places at the table of life. There is no 'harrassing struggle for existence.' They have enough for themselves and the stranger too. Those who are able, pay the fares of the children, or otherwise make some gift to the Society. . .and a little band of young wayfarers and homeless rovers in the world find themselves in comfortable and kind homes, with all the boundless advantages and opportunities of the western farmers life about them.[4]

It is evident that Brace had little understanding of rural conditions. For most midwestern farmers, life was a constant struggle, and, as he found out later, few were able to pay the children's fares or contribute to the Society. Nevertheless, he held out for his family plan. His arguments were persuasive enough to convince the Society, and on September 20, 1854, the first group of street children—forty-six boys and girls, ages ten to twelve—left New York City bound for the rural West.

Although this was the first "orphan train," the first leg of the journey was made by boat. They were given steerage passage upriver to Albany, from where a train would take them on to Dowagiac, Michigan.

The first problem to be encountered was one which no one seemed to have anticipated: The children were seasick! They arrived in Albany in various stages of queasiness. There they were forced to wait for six hours for the arrival of the train.

The children were chaperoned on this trip by two employees of the Children's Aid Society, E. P. Smith and C. R. Fry. The two of them, known as agents, worried during the long wait that Albany street boys might lure their young charges away. Despite some attempts, none of the orphans left the party, and one Albany boy was persuaded to join them.

When after six hours the train did arrive, other problems immediately arose. The children were to travel on an emigrant train, and though the conductor had promised that they would have a car to themselves, this did not happen. As agent Smith reported, "At the depot we worked our way through the Babel of at least one thousand Germans, Irish, Italians, and Norwegians, with whom nothing goes right." The minute the doors to the boxcars were opened, the immigrants rushed aboard, and Smith, Fry and the orphans were crowded in among all the others. "There were scenes that afternoon and night," Smith reported, "which it would not do to reveal. Irishmen passed around bad whiskey and sang bawdy songs; Dutch men and women smoked and sang, and grunted and cursed; babies squalled and nursed, and left no baby duties undone."[5] Night was the hardest part of the journey because of the total darkness of the boxcars and the lack of ventilation.

Morning improved the situation greatly. The children, many of whom had never seen farms or farm animals, were delighted with the country scenery near Rochester. "Each one must see everything we passed, find its name and make his own comments 'What's that, mister?' 'A cornfield.' 'Oh, yes, them's what make buckwheaters.' 'Look at them cows (oxen plowing) ; my mother used to milk cows.' As we whirled through orchards loaded with large, red apples, their enthusiasm rose to the highest pitch. It was difficult to keep them within doors."[6] When they finally reached their destination, the children were worn out from riding on the hard wooden benches, their clothes badly soiled and torn.

As they arrived in Dowagiac on a Sunday, they were greeted by the congregation of the Presbyterian church. When the services were over, it was discovered that one of the orphans had disappeared. However, by Monday evening the lost boy was found, and the placement of the children continued until, by the following Saturday, they were all in the homes of farm families.

Later, the Society organized local committees to screen foster parents in advance. But at this time, prospective parents had only to present recommendations from a pastor or the justice of the peace. Apparently, agent Smith felt no need to give a detailed account of the placement proceedings, as his report is casual and largely anecdotal. "I have great hopes for the majority of them," he wrote. "'Mag' is adopted by a wealthy Christian farmer. 'Smack,' the privateer from Albany, has a good home in a Quaker settlement. The two brothers, Dick and Jack, were taken by an excellent man and his son, living on adjacent farms. The German boy from the 'Lodging-house' lives with a physician in D—."[7]

Again in his report: "Several of the boys came in to see me, and tell their experiences in learning to farm. One of them was sure he knew how to milk, and being furnished with a pail, was told to take his choice of cows in the yard. He sprang for a two-year old steer, caught him by the horns, and called for a 'line to make him fast.'"[8]

Despite the fact that the first trip involved many difficulties (including the temporary loss of the small boy who wandered off and another boy who ran away because he wanted to be placed with a farmer rather than a tinker),

Children lined up to board an orphan train, ca. 1920.

Smith recommended that the Society send out more trains. "On the whole, the first experiment of sending children West is a very happy one, and I am sure there are places enough with good families in Michigan, Illinois, Iowa, and Wisconsin to give every poor boy and girl in New York a permanent home. The only difficulty is to bring the children to the homes."[9]

Smith's optimism was enough to convince the Children's Aid Society that the transportation of children should become a major endeavor, and despite criticism from many quarters, the trains began to leave for the Midwest on a regular basis.

Notes to Chapter 2

1. Peter Holloran, *Boston's Wayward Children: Social Services for Homeless Children, 1830-1930* (Cranbury, N. J.: Fairleigh Dickinson University Press, 1989), p. 45.

2. Miriam Z. Langsam, *Children West: A History of the Placing-Out System of the New York Children's Aid Society* (Madison, Wisconsin: State Historical Society of Wisconsin, 1964), p. 18.

3. Brace, *The Dangerous Classes of New York*, p. 415.

4. Brace, p. 232.   7. Brace, p. 252.

5. Brace, p. 249.   8. Brace, p. 253.

6. Brace, p. 250.   9. Brace, p. 254.

3: The Plan in Progress

THE LEGEND OF that first orphan train—the journey by boxcar—has persisted into recent times. In some areas, children who arrived on the orphan trains are still referred to by some as "boxcar children." This misconception may be due in part to *Orphan Train: A Novel*, published in 1967, and the television film based on the book.

The fact is that in the aftermath of that trip to Dowagiac, the Reverend Brace determined that thereafter the children should travel "by regular trains, in decent style," rather than by emigrant trains or boats. His procedure for placement was orderly and relatively simple. Each trainload of orphans was chaperoned by two agents, a man and a woman, employed by the Children's Aid Society. The Society sent notices in advance to the local postmaster, announcing the date and time of the train's arrival and the place where the children would be presented. Articles and advertisements in local newspapers described the terms under which children could be placed. Foster parents were screened in advance by a committee of prominent local citizens, usually ministers and businessmen.

On arrival the children were taken to a designated meeting place, such as a church, a hotel or the courthouse. If no other suitable area was available, the agents presented them at the depot. Many townspeople and farm families came to see the children simply out of curiosity. Some were looking for free labor. Others genuinely wanted to give a child a home.

It was both sad and amusing to learn that many agents apparently rehearsed the children in ways of attracting the attention of prospective parents. Some of the waifs ran to someone in the audience and asked plaintively to be taken. They are reported to have said something to the effect of "Please, could I be your little boy?" or "I want to be your

34

little girl." Some sang and danced. Such stories, as they were told to us by Rose Cranor and Alexander Douthit, another of the train riders, are common in the folklore of many towns along the orphan train routes.

Attached to the clothing of each of the children was a card, on the front of which was printed:

EMIGRATION DEPARTMENT
OF THE
Children's Aid Society of New York.
CENTRAL OFFICE UNITED CHARITIES BUILDING.
105 East 22nd Street, New York City.

The Society reserves the right to remove a child at any time for Just cause

Date of placing...
Name of Child...
Age...
B. W. Tice, Agent

The back of the card served as a contract between the Society and the foster parents:

Terms on which the Children are Placed in Homes
Applicants must be endorsed by the Local Committee.

The child selected may then be taken to the home for mutual acquaintance, but no permanent arrangements will be considered until the home has been visited by the Placing-Out Agent of the Society and the necessary papers signed.

Children under 14 years of age if not legally adopted, must be retained as members of the family, schooled according to the Educational Laws of the State, and comfortably clothed until they are 18 years old. It is then expected that suitable provision will be made for their future.

Children between 14 and 16 years of age must be boarded and clothed until they are 18 when they are at liberty to make their own arrangements.

Children over 16 years of age may be taken on a mutual agreement witnessed by the Agent of the Society or by a member of the local committee.

Parties taking children agree to make reports of them to the Society twice a year, and to urge the children to write also. Removals of children proving unsatisfactory can be arranged through the local committee or an Agent of the Society, the party agreeing to retain the child for a reasonable length of time after notifying the Society of the desired change.

As we can see by the last lines of the agreement, the child "proving unsatisfactory" is fairly easily removed. The foster parents are given some latitude in the decision. But nothing in the agreement gives the child much opportunity to change his mind. However, if the agent found the home unsatisfactory, he had the power to remove the child.

To a great extent the Society judged the children's welfare by their letters. It seems obvious that those who were happy and satisfied would be encouraged by their foster parents to write, while those who were not would be discouraged. Whenever possible the western agents visited the children on an annual basis and much of the information came from their reports.

A great part of the success of the placing-out system was due, as Brace readily acknowledged, to these agents, the various men and women who worked with the Society. Though Brace may have exaggerated somewhat in his accounts, certainly the agents' duties were many. Considering the methods of travel, the number of children on the trains, and the fact that two agents must supervise from twenty-five to thirty-five youngsters on each trip, it seems miraculous that the journeys went as smoothly as they apparently did. "It is a matter of devout thankfulness," Brace wrote at one point, "that no accident has ever happened to any one of the many parties of children we have sent out, or to the agents."[1] There is a later account of a little girl's broken leg, due to a fall. And doubtless there were minor mishaps. With thirty or so children on the train, running about at each stop, curious about everything in sight, there must have been many skinned shins and bumps and bruises with plenty of tears to go around.

Two of the placing-out agents mentioned by Brace were his brother, J. P. Brace, and E. Trott, whom he describes as "exceedingly able and judicious. . ." Their work enabled the Society's transportation policy to reach a new height at less

An early "agreement" between the Children's Aid Society and foster parents, signed by E. Trott.

expense than ever before. In 1871, for instance, more than three thousand children were sent out on the orphan trains at an expenditure of $31,638. This included train tickets and food as well as salaries for the agents. Aiding Trott and Brace was Charles R. Fry who, with E. P. Smith, had accompanied the first trainload of children in 1854.

Fry, a resident western agent, looked after "the interests of those previously sent," made annual visits to foster homes, and prepared the way for the next group. He traveled from town to town, explaining the work of the Society, arranging for local committees to screen foster parents, and sending out announcements. He appears to have been a man of great optimism and enthusiasm which never failed him. In 1869, arriving in Illinois with a trainload of orphans, he expressed once more the prevailing faith in the rural ideal. "Illinois is a beautiful country," he wrote. "All of the farmers seem to be wealthy. The larger boys, with two exceptions, were placed upon farms. Quite a number of boys came back to the hotel to say goodbye, and thanked me for bringing them out."[2]

At this time the Society was transporting children of any age. In Fry's party that year the ages ranged from one to twenty-one, the twenty-one-year-old being, in Fry's words, "the greatest babe of the company." As this boy was a musician, he played for the trainmen on the trip. At train stops, he played in saloons, where he urged the other boys to join him in entertaining customers for tips. Agent Fry, taking a dim view of such behavior, lectured his charges about it and found after a day or two that the musician had left the company, taking with him a concertina belonging to another boy. "The greatest babe" had caused so much trouble among the younger children and any adults he came in contact with that Fry was relieved to find him gone. "The most of my trouble seemed to take wing and fly away with him. He was the scapegoat of the party."

Although there are later reports of the difficulty of finding homes for handicapped children, Fry saw no problem at this time. With his usual rosy view of things, he seemed to find all the farmers sympathetic and well-to-do.

> One gentleman came in just for the purpose of seeing a little boy who had lost an eye, and was a brother to a boy his son had taken. When I told the little fellow that the gentleman lived near the man who had taken his brother, he climbed up on his knee, and putting his arms around his neck, said: 'I want to go home with you and be your boy; I want to see my brother.' The old gentleman wept, and wiping the tears from his eyes said: 'This is more than I can stand; I will take this boy home with me.'

He also cites a letter from a deaf-mute farmer who had taken a deaf-mute child.

> "C—— H——, Ind., March 5, 1860
>
> My Dear Sir—I received your kind letter some days ago. It has given me great pleasure to hear that you had arrived at your home. I got a report from you. The first of the time when you left D——, he cried and stamped on the floor by the door, but I took him to show him the horses; I told him when he will be a big man I would give him a horse. Then he quit crying and began to learn A, B, C, on that day when you left here. Now D—— is doing very well, and plays the most of anything; he likes to stay here very well; he can learn about dog and cat. I am willing to take care of him over twenty-one years old; then I will give him a horse, money, clothes,

school, etc. Last Saturday D—— rode on my colt himself; the colt is very gentle; on advice, he got off the colt; he petted the colt the most of the time; he likes to play with the young colt. He likes to stay with me, and he said he don't like to go back where you are. He gathers chips and fetches wood in the stove, and is willing to do all his work directly. I wonder that he bold boy and mock some neighbors.

Yours truly, friend,

L. F. W.

Write a letter to me immediately and let me know. He likes to go about with me, but not when it is very cold; I send him to stay in the house, out of the cold. When it is warm day, he likes to go about with me. Sometimes he goes to town. He pets the colt every day; sometimes he waters the colt and feed some corn himself.[3]

Agents such as Fry continued to function throughout the seventy-six year history of the orphan trains. Although relatively little is known of many of these men and women, we have fuller accounts of others. J. P. Brace served until his death in 1881. In *The Life of Charles Loring Brace*, written by his daughter Emma, she wrote of her uncle, "His affection for children made him a very kind caretaker during the long journeys and his tact and pleasant manners everywhere won friends for the cause. During his fifteen years of service, he had placed some ten thousand homeless children in homes. The long journeys were too great a strain and in the summer of 1881 he contracted a fever and died suddenly, leaving the 'home desolate of him who had made the homes of so many happy. His weary journeys in the cause of humanity are over. He sleeps in God.'" The last lines of the paragraph are quoted from the 29th Annual Report of the Children's Aid Society.

One of the best known and most active agents was the Reverend J. W. Swan. Born in Illinois in 1851, he moved to Nebraska with his parents at the age of four. In early adulthood he entered the Methodist ministry and served many churches in Nebraska until 1905. In 1903, while still active as a minister, he served as liason between the Children's Aid Society and the towns of that area. The following year, be-

The Rev. and Mrs. J. W. Swan, after their retirement in 1931. Shown with grandchildren. *(Courtesy Dorothea Swan Menke.)*

cause of his success in this rôle, the Society offered him a full-time position.

Swan's second wife, Hattie, also served as a western agent. Both seemed to have ideal temperaments for this work. To many children the Reverend Swan was always Grandpa Swan, remembered for his gentleness and sense of humor. In a 1986 interview, Noah Lawyer, recalling the trip west with his three brothers, said he remembered Swan as a short round man with a ready smile. "He was a very nice man." Others remember that Swan was very conscientious about visiting children every year or two after they were placed. On some occasions, when a child was found to be incompatible with his new family, he was taken by the Swans into their own home until a permanent home could be found.

A first-hand account of the Swans and their work comes from their daughter, Dorothea Swan Menke, of Sebastopol, California, who rode with her parents on one of the last of the orphan trains:

The year was 1927 and I was delegated to make the trip to New York with my parents to bring a company of children to Palmyra, Missouri, for placement. (This was my graduation gift.) We took the trip on the Missouri Pacific Rail Road as it ran out of Sedalia and my parents were given passes on this line as well as the M K & T—so this was called Katy RR.

It was shortly after we arrived in New York and were on the bus when there were a lot of horn honking and then we saw a plane and we learned this was Charles Lindberg [sic] when he made his non-stop transatlantic flight. There were small pieces of paper (resembling bills) flying everywhere and people picking them up. It was an exciting thing to see.

I cannot remember much about the Orphanage building. It did not seem large to me. The smaller children were all sleeping in individual beds in one room. I cannot remember any tour of the Orphanage. Everything looked nice and clean.

In our company there were ten or eleven children, ranging in ages from 3 to 12 or so. The children looked nice and I am sure they were pleased to know they were taking a long train ride. They were well behaved and seemed to enjoy themselves on the train trip. We ate some hot meals and a few snacks. It seems to me we slept in the chairs but am not sure. If the train stop was long enough for us to go outside we tried to walk together. My father had a lot of dry wit and to see that many children people would ask him if they were all his. He replied yes, they are in my care. Then he would smile and tell his story. When we arrived at Palmyra we went directly to the Theatre. Everything seemed to move smoothly. I think the homes had been visited and chosen if children suited the people who were to take them. Some visited with the children before their mind was made up but all the children in that company were placed. If the new parents could take 2 of a family it was good and then if more in that family they would try to place the rest in that Community so the children could keep in touch. Visits were made shortly after placement to see if all was going well and if a child must be removed for some reason (usually they came to our house to stay until a new place was found for them). I think a number of visits were made the first year to see that all was going well. My parents said they wanted the children placed where they were loved and were one of the family. Follow-up visits were important also. As I recall most of the company did continue in those homes. Years after placement I remember during my early years some of the children would come by and this was always a joy to my parents.

Dorothea Menke

P.S. I should mention we went to the Recreation Hall or Theatre in Palmyra, and the children went in a group on the stage and the names were called so the new parents would know their child. It went smoothly and certainly did not take long.[4]

When the Reverend Swan died at his home in Sedalia in 1934, his work with the orphan trains was prominently mentioned in the obituaries. Newspapers and Sedalia residents recalled this work as his finest achievement. One of the stories repeated among the residents is that of a little girl who could not be placed because of her disfigured face. The Swans adopted her as their daughter Elsie. Another story is that the Swans would at times have as many as seventeen children living with them.

Less is known of another Missouri agent, Miss Georgia Greenleaf. We do know that she had relatives and friends in Laclede County, Missouri, in the area of Lebanon. Often, if no permanent home could be found for the children, Miss Greenleaf would place them temporarily with her friends or relatives, rather than return them to New York. She is remembered by some of those who came on trains as a lady of great kindness and devotion, who took her work with the orphans as a life's calling.

Even less is known of other western agents. But the Society has no documents criticizing them, and the orphans in their recollections are unanimous in their praise of those dedicated men and women.

Notes to Chapter 3

1. Brace, *The Dangerous Classes of New York*, p. 268.
2. Brace, p. 256.
3. Brace, p. 257.
4. Dorothea Swan Menke, letter to Evelyn Sheets, July 21, 1985.

4: Criticisms, Flaws and Defenses

AS THE PRACTICE of transporting children continued, a number of changes were made in the placing-out system. Having learned from Fry's experience with the twenty-one-year-old who had made so much trouble, it was decided that no young adults should be taken. Nor would they take any very young children. Exceptions did occur, but the preferred ages ranged from five to twelve. Both the Society and the foster families were finding that youngsters of this age group could do some work on the farms and more easily adjust to becomng members of the family.

Another change was the decision to pick up no more children along the way. Only those who were aboard when the trains left New York would be taken to the destined stops.

Although a third policy change was not explicitly stated, later reports show that it did become a practice: the Society no longer referred to the farmers and others who took the children as employers. Emphasis was placed on the concept of the foster *parent*, and on adoption.

It may be noted here that of nearly forty train riders whose stories have come to us, either first-hand or through members of their families, only eight were legally adopted. Though the reasons varied from family to family, legal and court fees were usually a factor. Many families simply could not afford them. And there was often among the rural folk the common suspicion of lawyers, who were to be avoided whenever possible, and of courts in general. In some cases, where the child was considered a real part of the family, legal papers just didn't seem necessary.

In spite of refinements, the good work and dedication of the agents, and the genuine compassion which was Brace's abiding motivation, his plan for placing children in the West

Children's Aid Society,

(PLACING-OUT DEPARTMENT,)

United Charities Building,   **105 EAST 22nd STREET, NEW YORK.**

I, the undersigned, *J. D. Creath*
hereby agree to provide for *Fredrick Inph*
now of the age of ___*6*___ years, until the said boy shall
reach the age of 18 years, according to the following terms and conditions, and with the full understanding that the Society reserves the right to
remove the child previous to legal adoption if at any time the circumstances
of the home become such as in the judgment of the agent are injurious to the
physical, mental or moral well-being of the child.

The terms and the conditions for the retention of the boy in my family
being as follows:—To care for him in sickness and in health, to send him
to school during the entire free school year until he reaches the age of 14
years, and thereafter during the winter months at least, until he reaches the
age of 16 years; also to have him attend Church and Sunday School
when convenient, and to retain him as a member of my family until he
reaches the age of 17 years, and thereafter for the final year, until he is
18 years old, to pay the boy monthly wages in addition to his mainte-
nance, the amount thereof to be previously determined after consultation with
the Society's local agent and his approval. In case he proves unsatisfactory, I agree to notify the Society, and pending his removal, to keep him a
reasonable length of time after such notice has been given. I agree, more-
over, to use my best endeavor then and at all times, to detain him, should
he try to leave me, until the Society can take steps for his removal. I
agree to keep him at all times as well supplied with clothing as he was when
I received him.

I agree to write to the Society at least once a year, and should I
change my address I will notify the Society.

Witness, *J. W. Swan*
Adriance Jno.

Date, *Dec 15* ___1913

A later agreement between the Children's Aid Society and foster parents.

met with early and continuing opposition. Arguments against it were many and varied. Some critics thought the plan a Protestant plot to convert Catholic or Jewish children. Others believed it to be a system of involuntary servitude, providing farmers with free labor. Certain New York civic leaders and factory owners believed the plan robbed the city of a source of cheap labor and its youth. An article in the *New York Journal of Commerce,* May 24, 1879, maintained that the Society, in its professed claim of alleviating juvenile delinquency, was sending out not the worst boys but the healthiest and strongest. Various opponents of the trains raised the question of child abuse. Even the matter of incest became an issue because of the fear that brothers and sisters reared in separate homes might unknowingly marry.

In the Midwest there was some fear of intermarriage in general, between native sons and daughters and orphans of unknown origin. The fear was probably compounded by the features and complexion of New York orphans, many of whom were of swarthy central European stock. This was especially true of those from the third wave of immigration.

It was probably in an effort to appease the prejudices of the panicky few that several states passed legislation censuring the Children's Aid Society for its transportation policy. As early as 1901 the Missouri General Assembly passed the following law:

CRIMES AND PUNISHMENTS: Importation of Children.

AN ACT to prohibit the importation into this state by corporations or individuals of afflicted, indigent and vicious children, with an emergency clause.

SECTION
1. State board of charities and for violation corrections shall authorize importation of children.

SECTION
2. Penalty

3. Emergency clause

Be it enacted by the General Assembly of the State of Missouri, as follows:

SECTION 1. No association incorporated under the laws of any other state than that of Missouri shall place any child in any family within the boundaries of the state of Missouri, either with or without indenture, or for adoption, unless the said association shall have furnished the state board of charities and corrections with such guarantee as they may require that no child shall be brought into the state of Missouri by such society or its agents having any contagious or incurable disease or being of feeble mind or vicious character, and that said association will promptly receive and remove from the state any child brought into the state of Missouri by its agents which shall become a public charge within the period of five years after being brought into this state.

SEC. 2. Any person who shall receive to be placed in a home, or shall place in a home any child in behalf of any association incorporated in any other state than the state of Missouri, which shall not have complied with the requirements of the preceeding section shall, upon conviction, be punished by imprisonment in jail not more than thirty days, or by fine of not less than five or more than one hundred dollars, or by both such fine and imprisonment.

SEC. 3. The necessity of this act going into effect at once on account of the fact that the New York children's aid society is pouring car loads of children into the state without properly supervising them, thereby burdening our commonwealth, creates an emergency within the meaning of the constitution; therefore, this act shall take effect and be enforced from and after its passage.

Approved March 13, 1901.

The bill was introduced by Senator John Clay of St. Francois County, one of the more rural areas of the state, almost a model for the kind of place Brace considered ideal for the children.

The penalties for violation of the law were not so severe as the tone of the bill would lead us to expect. As far as can be determined the law was never enforced.

Throughout, Brace continued to believe in his plan and defended it with arguments of his own.

If your son suddenly, by the death of his parents and relatives, were to be thrown out on the streets, poor and homeless—as these children are—would you prefer him to be placed—in an Asylum, or in a good farmer's home in the West?
The plainest farmer's home rather than the best Asylum—a thousand times was always my sincere answer.[1]

Health certificate for Billy Czik (Willie Paul Dunnaway). All children received medical examinations before transportation.

Many of the charges against the plan were unjustified. But there were indeed real flaws which were never completely mended. To begin with, the Society underestimated the number of children they would have to cope with. They had expected at first to be receiving only true orphans. As it turned out, many of the street arabs or the children who crowded the orphanages had one parent living and sometimes both and had been turned out strictly for lack of funds to support them. This swelled the ranks of the homeless with whom the Society was trying to cope.

There was no great lack of families wishing to adopt a child. All the charitable institutions in the city had a waiting list of prospective foster parents. The problem was that all of them wanted only a certain type of child. "It is a two-year old, blue-eyed golden haired little girl with curls. That is the order that everybody leaves. It cannot be filled fast enough."[2] This left thousands of others who must be cared for in one way or another.

Considering the overwhelming numbers, certain lapses in the plan may well be understood. Probably because of its white, Anglo-Saxon nature, the Children's Aid Society did not openly concern itself with black or Oriental children. Brace, being a practical man, may well have recognized that placing such children in the Midwest or in the South, among predominantly Anglo-Saxon Protestant families, would be difficult if not downright impossible. It is to be remembered that the orphan trains began in 1854, when the issue of slavery was about to divide the nation, and continued throughout the conflict. Brace could hardly have been blind to the fact that placement of black orphans could lead to accusations that the Society was promoting involuntary servitude, sending out little children to be slaves. The usual procedure was to send them instead to an orphans' home, often in Baltimore.

Prudent though the Society seems to have been, in the history and lore of many midwestern families there are stories of children from racial, ethnic and religious minorities who came on the trains. From Mrs. Elizabeth Senger Mann of Broken Arrow, Oklahoma, we learn of an instance in her family:

> My aunt, Rachel Marie Donnivan Senger was one of the orphans. She was adopted by my grandparents in Pierce City, Lawrence County, Missouri. She was born in New York about 1892. She died at the age of 67. I am interested in finding out more about her family. She was four years old when my grandparents got her. They never mentioned it. I was a teenager before I knew she was adopted. She was always one of the family. She had some negro blood but that was never mentoned. I only

learned this from my friend's mother when I was in High School.[3]

As for religious background, Brace was apparently so eager to place children that he required only that the home be Christian. Catholic children were sometimes entrusted to Catholic families. But quite often they were given to whatever family would take them and made members of whatever denomination the family belonged to. The denominations ranged from the major ones to minorities such as Quakers.

Occasionally Jewish children were placed in Christian homes. In the course of our interviews we came across one such instance in Missouri. According to Mary Hamilton Bracken Phillips of Blackwater, a Jewish boy grew up in her father's home. "When I asked [my father] where he came from, father said he didn't know. The boy about twelve just got off the train and walked up the hill. His mother brought the boy home. I asked what his name was, Father said he took the name Bracken." Though family history is vague about the boy, Mrs. Phillips' brother, who died in 1984, said he thought the boy's first name was Sam, and he later lived in Blackwater, Saline County, Missouri. Mrs. Phillips is still searching for further information about him.[4]

To Brace and the Society religious differences were secondary to the ideal of the rural environment. But the question of religion continued to disturb the critics. One of the staunch defenders of the policy was John Macy, the assistant secretary of the Society, who in 1871 was directly involved with the placement and supervision of the children. His rôle was to handle correspondence with eight to ten thousand people. He answered about two thousand letters a year from children or the adults with whom they had been placed. Judging by Macy's correspondence, the Society argued that of twenty-one thousand children sent on the orphan trains by 1871 only twelve had turned out to be criminals; the number who ran away was too small to count; and the "system of sending [children of the same families] to the West [was] one of the best features of the Society."[5]

However, even with a firm commitment to the policy, John Macy still felt a need to defend it against criticisms that it allowed the religion of the children, and sometimes their names, to be changed. He testified that name changes never occurred and that "Catholic children had often been intrusted to Catholic families." But his testimony hedges the question somewhat. The Society did not prohibit the foster parents from changing a child's last name and sometimes the first name as well. It seems to have been a common practice, without consulting the child. And though Catholic children often were placed with Catholic families, this was not always the case.

Bellevue Hospital, which also had a placing-out policy, had a simple method of settling the Catholic-Protestant question. When a baby was taken in, they kept it for one day, then sent it either to the Protestant Infant Asylum or the New York Foundling Hospital. In a 1907 issue of *The Delineator,* then edited by Theodore Dreiser, Mabel Potter Daggett wrote: "Babies are made Protestants or Catholics alternately as they are received and their lives are directed accordingly."[6]

It was probably in reaction to such a system that in 1869 the Sisters of Charity of St. Vincent de Paul established the Catholic Charities of New York, through the New York Foundling Hospital. The Sisters had always taken in abandoned babies. In the main hall of the hospital they kept a cradle, where mothers could leave their newborn infants anonymously. But soon they had more children than they could accommodate. Following the example of the orphan trains, the hospital established the Catholic mercy trains and through priests of the Midwest and South began to send children to foster homes.

There was a major difference in the Catholic policy. The Children's Aid Society found homes for the children *after* the trains arrived at their destinations. The mercy trains carried only those who had been assured of homes *before* the trains left New York. This way, the children knew they were wanted before they were taken from the orphanage. (As is noted later, even this policy had its occasional failures.)

Another difference was the Catholic indenture, a much longer legal statement than the Children's Aid Society's card, though both statements cover the same details in regard to room, board, clothing, medical care, education and supervision, the first part of the Catholic contract refers to the laws of the State of New York under which the child is indentured.

Article II requires that the child be instructed in the Catholic faith and be "treated with care and tenderness as if he were in fact the child of the parties of the second part. . ." Article IV requires that the foster parents report to the Board of Managers, in writing, at least every six months. Article VIII, the final article, differs substantially from the Society's contract in that it establishes the child's rights of inheritance. It provides that, whether the child is legally adopted or not, if he has lived with the foster parents until he is twenty-one, he shall inherit the property of his foster parents "as if he had been the natural and legitimate child of the parties of the second part."

For the journey on the Catholic trains, each child wore a suit or dress made by the Sisters, with the child's name pinned on the inside and the name of the new parents pinned inside the back of the collar. Often the Protestant children on the Children's Aid Society trains also wore uniforms from the orphanages. Rose Cranor, who came on an orphan train, never lost or disposed of the little dress she wore on the journey. Now after her death the dress is an heirloom treasured by her daughter Bedonna Rice.

Although religious differences were a major issue among critics of Brace's plan, they were not, as nearly as we have found, of any great concern to the children themselves. The children had other problems. And here we come to the system's most glaring flaw: the emotional distress of the homeless young, which certain aspects of the plan often caused. Most of the children had lost one or both of their parents. The street arabs had suffered hunger, cold, disease and abuse. All of them had been uprooted from the urban life they were accustomed to and set down in a rural world completely foreign to them. As a final blow, they were usually separated from brothers and sisters, placed alone among strangers.

A humanitarian in every other sense, Brace apparently was not sensitive to the significance of the biological family. This is made quite clear in his response to objections raised by Professor Henry Fawcett, who published *Pauperism: Its Cures and Remedies* in 1871. Fawcett complained that street urchins were receiving better treatment than children of the working poor who tried to take care of their own. Brace replied that ". . .we are perfectly ready to do the same for the outside, hard-working poor; but their attachment to the city, their ignorance or bigotry, and their affection for their children, will always prevent them from use of such benefaction to any large degree."[7] In other words, the poor parents' love for their young was a handicap! If those children were kept at home, they were denied what Brace considered the greater benefits of rural life.

Here again we come to Brace's romantic notion of rustic bliss, a misconception which contributed to the separation of siblings. The rural Midwest may have been, to his mind, a land of milk and honey. But the milk and honey were hard-earned and rather more meager than Brace and his agents would believe. Though many farmers saw the orphans as more hands to help with the hard work, few could afford to take more than one. The separation of children of the same family was an inevitable and routine procedure.

Furthermore, it seems never to have occurred to Brace that the orphans might be happier in an orphanage or in any familiar environment—dirty, crowded, noisy though it might be—than in the wholesome countryside. As we found in the course of our research, some of them were.

The twin sisters, Dorothy and Susan Bond, were six years old when they were placed in an orphanage in Brooklyn. "They were the happiest days of my life," Susan Bond wrote in 1985. "On every Saturday we went to the Brooklyn Bridge for a walk or to Coney Island. We then went home and had our usual meal, ginger snaps and milk. On Sundays we went to Trinity Church for services. . .The day we were to leave Mr. Swan of Sedalia, Missouri, came after us. We were checked by a doctor, given a bath, new clothes and both of us crying for we didn't want to leave. With Mr. Swan we went to the train and cried all the way to Vandalia, [Missouri]."[8]

In their zeal, Brace and his colleagues seemed to have been oblivious to or chose to ignore the many emotional problems which their policies might cause the children.

Written and oral records clearly reveal the state of mind of those orphans suddenly removed from noisy, crowded streets to the isolation of the farms. For most of them the train trip was their first glimpse of rural life. Their emotions ranged from delight to awe to fear, as they saw the changing scenery—orchards, fields of grain and pasture land with grazing cattle and horses. Then came the separations. As the train crossed the country it left part of its cargo at each stop, a few here, a few there, until all the children had been claimed. And so began a new, strange and sometimes lonely life.

Aside from the anguish of separation, one of the worst experiences the children had to endure was the fear that no family would take them. Youngsters with physical disfigurement or even a slightly disabling injury were at particular risk. To stand before an audience time after time as the train moved westward, to wait hopefully and not be chosen, was a misery which no child who had suffered through it would soon forget.

It happened at times that when an orphan train arrived at a scheduled stop, there were not enough generous adults at the meeting place to take all the children. In this case, the Society's placing-out agent often remained in the community for several days, looking for homes for those not selected. If none could be found, the child traveled on to other stops or was returned with the agent to New York.[9]

Most of the children who were chosen seem to have lived happy lives. But there were exceptions. We came across one such case, that of Mary Goth, whom we located in 1985 in a nursing home in Clinton, Missouri. At that time Mary was ninety-three years old. Her memory was excellent. Recalling her early years she said, "My experience was that of a servant. My foster mother was cruel—Oh, she was a crackerjack. They wanted one of the sons to get me pregnant so I'd stay home and work." The idea was so outrageous and the family so harsh that Mary left them and went out to support herself. Mary Goth died in 1989, but she is remembered by many in Clinton as a woman of kindness and courage.

Another of the unfortunates was a little girl named Marian Burke, who arrived in Taos, Missouri, in Cole County, on a mercy train. She was two years old. Many years later, in 1986, her daughter, Mrs. Geraldine Bass, now living in Olathe, Kansas, wrote of her mother:

> The family who adopted her were childless until she arrived. They had a child of their own the following year. They abused my mother because they no longer wanted her. She had a scar on her left arm the size of an iron.

The mother scalded her on purpose. She remembers very little about her life during this time except the bad things. . .

They were so cruel to her that another family in town took her away from them and treated her as one of the family for the rest of their lives. She was treated very kindly and grew up to be one of the sweetest, most pleasant people you could ever know. She was truly loved by all who knew her. . .

So often you hear that children who are abused go on to abuse their own children. She treated us with love and affection our entire lives. I always felt that she lived her childhood over again thru our childhoods. She had three children, all girls. She was my best friend.[10]

One of the saddest stories comes from Mrs. Mina Hess of Kansas City, who grew up on a farm in Northern Minnesota.

As a preschool child I remember that we had a family who went to the Twin Cities to get one of these orphans to help with the farm chores. The farmers had five small children so he (the orphan) had to help in the home also.

At age sixteen he was allowed to leave to seek his own fortune elsewhere. One day he came to our home to bid goodbye to my parents. We had just finished dinner. My mother fixed a good dinner spread for him. He ate as though he was real hungry, and talked to my parents about the abuse and beatings he had suffered; also that he had to eat scraps in the kitchen when the family was in the dining room.

He did not know where he was going to find a job but he was going to town to hitch a ride on a freight train. My mother packed a lunch for him and asked him to come and see us. Here his reply was 'I'd like to come back and beat up that man who has mistreated me.' This reply made an impression on my young mind as he seemed small and thin, blond and very nice looking. My parents and siblings prayed that God would take care of him. We never saw nor heard from him.[11]

Overlooking the damage to the children which the system might and sometimes did cause, the Reverend Brace continued to follow his convictions. He recognized early enough, however, that in order to silence his critics and raise money, he would have to produce both statistical and anecdotal evidence of the success of the trains. The following is an extract from his 1859 report to the Children's Aid Society:

During the last spring, the secretary made an extended journey through the Western States, to see for himself the nature and results of this work, carried on for the last five years through those States, under Mr. Tracy's careful supervision. During that time we have scattered several thousands of poor boys and girls. In this journey he visited personally, and heard directly of, many hundreds of these little creatures, and appreciated for the first time, to the fullest extent, the spirit with which the West has opened its arms to them. The effort to reform and improve these young outcasts has become a mission-work there. Their labor, it is true, is needed. But many a time a bountiful and Christian home is opened to the miserable little stranger, his habits are patiently corrected, faults without number are borne with, time and money are expended on him, solely and entirely from the highest religious motive of a noble self-sacrifice for an unfortunate fellow-creature. The peculiar warm-heartedness of the Western people, and the equality of all classes, give them an especial adaption to this work, and account for their success.

'Wherever we went (we quote from [Tracy's] account) we found the children sitting at the same table with the families, going to school with the children, and every way treated as well as any other children. Some whom we had seen once in the most extreme misery, we beheld sitting, clothed and clean, at hospitable tables, calling the employer, "father," loved by the happy circle, and apparently growing up with as good hopes and prospects as any children in the country. Others who had been in the city on the very line between virtue and vice, and who at any time might have fallen into crime, we saw pursuing industrial occupations, and gaining a good name for themselves in their village. The observations on this journey alone would have rewarded years of labor for this class. The results—so far as we could ascertain them—were remarkable, and, unless we reflect on the wonderful influences possible from a Christian home upon a child unused to kindness, they would almost seem incredible.'

The estimate we formed from a considerable field of observation was, that, out of those sent to the West under fifteen years, not more than two per cent, turned out bad; and, even of those from fifteen to eighteen, not more than four per cent.[12]

While criticism of the orphan trains was not silenced, the Society continued to seek ways of measuring its work.

During the 1870s the transportation of children was at its height, with over three thousand being sent each year to the Midwest and the South. Brace noted that in this period New York City police statistics showed a great decrease in arrests of juveniles for thievery, petty larceny, and female vagrancy, as well as fewer boys imprisoned as pickpockets. At a time when the population of New York was increasing at the rate of 13.5 percent, this decrease in the crime rate, Brace concluded, was a direct result of the trains.

In 1898 Brace's son Robert surveyed the children from fifteen groups placed in Iowa, northern Missouri, eastern Nebraska and Kansas. He concluded that 90 percent were doing well. The Society in its report of 1900 stated that the records of all the younger children placed in foster homes up to that time showed that 87 percent were doing well. The statistics are somewhat suspect, however. The groups surveyed did not include teen-agers who had been "placed in situations at wages," because these older children were hard to keep track of.

A few years later Mabel Potter Daggett defended the placement policy in her *Delineator* article. "The Children's Aid Society have a list of great lawyers, mayors, and congressmen taken from the streets of New York." She then presents what she calls "the best story of all," that of two boys, eight and nine years old, who had been committed to the city's institution for children, then on Randall's Island. One of the boys was found wandering in Chatham Square by President Roosevelt's father. In 1859 both boys were taken to Indiana on an orphan train and placed on separate farms. Both worked their way through school and college. Barely thirty years later, in 1890, one of them, Andrew H. Burke, became the first governor of North Dakota. The other, John J. Brady, graduated from Yale and was appointed by President McKinley as governor of Alaska.

To Daggett the orphan trains, the mercy trains and the other charitable policies for the care of unwanted street children represented "an insurance against crime."[13]

As further proof of the policy's effectiveness, the two governors were mentioned again in the Society's annual report for 1917. They head a list of orphan train riders who had become eminently successful.

A Governor of a State, A Governor of a Territory, two members of Congress, two District Attorneys, two Sheriffs, two Mayors, a Justice of the Supreme Court, four Judges, two college professors, a cashier of an insurance company, twenty-four clergymen, seven high school Principals, two School Superintendents, an Auditor-General of the State, nine members of State Legislatures, two artists, a Senate Clerk, six railroad officials, eighteen journalists, thirty-four bankers, nineteen physicians, thirty-five lawyers, twelve postmasters, three contractors, ninety-seven teachers, four civil engineers, and any number of business and professional men, clerks, mechanics, farmers, and their wives, and others who have acquired property and filled positions of honor and trust. Nor would the roll call be complete without mention of four army officers and 7,000 soldiers and sailors in their country's service.

It would seem that despite its shortcomings, the plan was succeeding in the face of all opposition.

Notes to Chapter 4

1. Brace, *The Dangerous Classes of New York*, p. 237.
2. Daggett, "The Child Without a Home," p. 510.
3. Elizabeth Senger Mann, letter to Michael Patrick, May 25, 1987.
4. Mary Hamilton Bracken Phillips, letter to Michael Patrick, July 15, 1987.
5. Brace, p. 269.
6. Daggett, p. 508.
7. Brace, p. 266.
8. Susan Bond, letter to Evelyn Sheets, 1985.
9. Miriam Z. Langsam, *Children West*, pp. 23-24.
10. Geraldine Bass, letter to Evelyn Trickel, October 20, 1986.
11. Mina Hess, letter to Evelyn Trickel, November 14, 1986.
12. Brace, p. 249.
13. Daggett, p. 508.

5: A Special Case

Much of this story is told in a series of letters which passed between representatives of the Children's Aid Society and Mr. and Mrs. George E. Woodruff, both of whom were attorneys practicing in Trenton, Missouri. The interchange of messages, over a period of four years, gives an interesting insight into the work of the Society and the concern of all for the well-being of the children. Because of this, we have included here all the existing correspondence regarding this particular case. Permission for use of the letters comes from Dorothy Weir Davidson. (The letters appear in their original form, the spelling, punctuation and grammar that of the correspondents.)

In the late 1920s three children named Weir were sent to Trenton, Missouri, on orphan trains. They arrived separately, at different times. Billy, the youngest, was only two years old. From his older sister Dorothy, now Mrs. John Davidson, we have an account of his placement and that of their sister Phyllis:

> My brother came with a group of very young children before the train [on which I came]. How I do not know, but they called Mrs. Woodruff and said they had this little boy (2 years) that they needed to have a home for the night. She wasn't very interested, but she went and took a look and took him home for the night and that was all it took. They kept him.
> The Children's Aid Society knew Mr. and Mrs. Woodruff wanted a girl so they wrote a letter to the Woodruffs that they had a little girl that was the sister to the boy they had, and would they be interested on a trial basis. They were and they sent her down.
> Later some way Mrs. Woodruff's sisters met Phyllis and Billy, and they thought Phyllis had colored blood

in her, because of her dark coloring and flat nose (she was born without a bridge in her nose).

The Woodruffs, "with the seed of doubt" in their minds, decided to send Phyllis back to New York. They notified the agent of the Children's Aid Society, the Reverend J. W. Swan, and at this point the exchange of letters begins. The first of these still in existence comes from the Reverend Swan, written by hand and dated October 11, 1930.

Dear Friend.

We were very sorry that we did not have time to talk with you longer at the depot concerning Phyllis. Mrs. Swan is planning to go east in a few days to return one of her girls. If you do not want to keep Phyllis let know at once. Mrs. Swan will go as soon as she can hear from the office. If you dont want Phyllis wire us at once & I'll wire you when you bring her to Chillochothe. I'll take the girl Phyls [sic] to meet Mrs. Swan. She will go from Omaha to Chicago. Would you be willing to pay Phyllis fare to Chicago? If so have her ready to put [illegible] the train as I go through Chillocothe. Wire as soon as you get this your decision. In haste—

Most. Respt.
J. W. Swan

Though we do not have the Woodruffs' reply, apparently it was prompt, as on November 24, in another handwritten letter, Swan apologizes for not answering sooner.

Dear Friends

Yours of 15th inst. rec'd. We have been absent from home visiting our sons in Neb. Came home Saturday a. m. I hasten a reply. Very sorry that you have determined to give up Phylis. According to our promise we will remove her. Just what we can do with her we are at a loss to know. We will take the matter up immediately with the office & let you know as soon as we get a reply. Could you not make inquiry among your friends, perhaps someone would like to have her. If you know of a good home let her go and stay with them until we can hear from the office. If you can find a home or take Phillis until we can adjust the matter. Mrs. Swan went to New York since we saw you. She would have taken Phillis

59

with her if you had not decided to keep her. In haste

Most. Respt.
Mr. and Mrs. J. W. Swan

Soon after that November letter, the little girl was indeed sent back to New York. But the Woodruffs "missed her so much after having her for awhile" that she was scarcely gone before the Children's Aid Society received a telegram: "Return Phyllis Weir with Mr. Swan and we will keep her for sure."

On December 23 Miss Helen Baxter, a Society supervisor, wrote to the Woodruffs:

Upon receipt of your telegram Saturday, Mrs. Swan started west with Phyllis and by now she must be reestablished in your home. I was glad that you felt that you wanted her back because it will be so nice for the children to grow up together. I am afraid Phyllis' future would not have been anywhere near as happy had she not been returned.

It seemed only fair to ask you to pay for Phyllis' ticket east and back to you again. The cost of the two tickets amounts to $23.50.

With best wishes for a happy holiday season, I am

Yours most sincerely,
Helen Baxter
Superintendent

So little Phyllis, of the dark coloring and flat nose, was back home in time for Christmas.

Immediately following Phyllis' return there were several letters concerning the railroad fare. The Woodruffs wrote Miss Baxter, asking that they be allowed to delay payment of the $23.50. Her reply is dated January 6, 1931.

My dear Mrs. Woodruff:

Thank you very much for your letter of the 1st.

It will be all right for you to send the money for Phyllis' ticket later. We only charged you for her ticket but did not include any of the other expenses incurred on account of the trip east and back again.

We are, of course, all delighted that you wanted Phyllis back again and more so to know how much you found you thought of her. Every body has told me that she is a very sweet child and it is nice to know that she has completely won her way into your hearts.

With best wishes to you all for a very happy New Year, I am

> Yours sincerely,
> Helen Baxter
> Superintendent

The next letter is dated January 27, 1931.

The Children's Aid Society
105 East 22nd Street,
New York City

Dear Miss Baxter:

Enclosed find check for $23.50 in payment of the two tickets for Phyllis' transportation.

We thank you again for all favors in regard to the matter, and with best wishes, we are

> Respectfully yours,
> Woodruff & Woodruff

Miss Baxter acknowledged receipt on January 29.

My dear Mrs. Woodruff:

Thank you very much, indeed, for your note of 27th enclosing the check for $23.50.

While you did not say so, I feel sure that Phyllis is getting along nicely as ever with you and you are still happy having her back again.

With best wishes to you all, I am

> Yours sincerely,
> Helen Baxter
> Superintendent

It was less than a month after Miss Baxter's letter that the third Weir child came to live with the Woodruffs. Dorothy, sometimes called Dora, had come to Trenton on an orphan train in the spring of 1929. On April 17, the following story appeared in the Trenton *Republican-Times:*

ORPHAN CHILDREN ARE NOW IN HOMES
Three Girls Brought Here on Last Trip,
Have Been Replaced, Swan States

The nine boys brought here for adoption by Mr. and

Mrs. J. T. [sic] Swan, the former of whom is the Missouri agent for the Children's Aid Society of New York, have all been placed in homes, and Mr. and Mrs. Swan will leave for their home in Sedalia, Mo., tomorrow, it was learned today.

Ellas Huzar, 14 years old, has been placed in the care of C. D. Axtel, a mile from town where he can continue his high school education.

William French, 13, has been taken by Mr. and Mrs. Fred S. Dickman, John McDonald, 10, has been placed with Mr. and Mrs. Elton R. Davis.

Gerald Doty, 5, has been taken by Mr. and Mrs. A. B. Fear of Tindall, Peter Newman, 9, has been taken by Mr. and Mrs. H. C. Smith at Galt, and his brother, Edward Newman, 8, has been placed with Mr. and Mrs. L. C. Hatcher, also at Galt, the last being a temporary placement according to Mr. Swan.

Three children placed here on his former trip have also been replaced, Mr. Swan said. They are Martha Shepherd, 14, who has a home now with Mr. and Mrs. Perry H. Rhea, of Trenton, Clara Shepherd, 9, who is with Mr. and Mrs. H. W. Boysal, and Dora Weir, 5, who has been placed with Mr. and Mrs. William A. Wingate.

Few here will dispute the children, as placed are all in fine homes and Mr. and Mrs. Swan have done all in their power to see all of the children have been well located.

Dorothy (or Dora) Weir remained with the Wingates until February of the following year. At about that time Mrs. Wingate left her husband. Not sure whether or not she would come back, Mr. Wingate asked the Woodruffs to look after Dorothy for a while. From there on letters fly thick and fast between the Woodruffs, the Swans and representatives of the Children's Aid Society. February 18, 1931—Woodruffs to J. W. Swan:

Dear Mr. Swan:

We have your letter of several weeks ago. Kindly pardon us for not answering sooner.

After talking with Mr. Wingate, and after several visits by Dorothy with us since your letter, we have decided, if it meets with your approval, that we want Dorothy, at least on trial. She is more than willing and the children too are anxious for her. She visited us yesterday afternoon staying for supper, and when Mr. Wingate came for her, she begged him to let her stay—she said she

Dorothy (Dora) Weir, age five or six. *(Courtesy Dorothy Weir Davidson.)*

wanted to stay all the time. It was only after my telling her to get ready and go with her daddy, that she consented. Of course, she thinks all the world of her daddy, but as you stated in your letter, she needs a mother.

We believe that it will be to the best interest of all [three of the children] that they be in the same home. Of course, we would want Dorothy on trial, although from the three visits she has made to us during the past two weeks, we have no doubt of her being satisfactory as far as she is concerned. Of course we have to consider the financial side of the matter—as far as the trouble concerned, that will amount to very little, as I find Billy and Phyllis no trouble at all. Of course, Phyllis practically cares for herself and does a lot for us too, and is so willing. Dorothy seems to be just as nice a child as Billy and Phyllis and we are very anxious for her. If the above application meets with your approval, kindly send word to Mr. Wingate to turn her over to us, which I think he will take very kindly from his talk with us, or if you think necessary, you might come yourself and make the change.

With best wishes to you and Mrs. Swan, we are

> Yours respectfully.
> WOODRUFF & WOODRUFF
> By ....

February 19, 1931—Mr. and Mrs. Swan to the Woodruffs:

Dear Friends:

Your letter recd. We were somewhat surprised at your proposition to take Dorothy into your family. I am quite sure you are assuming quite a responsibility. If we do not assume any responsibility, we will not be able to accomplish much in live [*sic*]. I can conceive [no] more *noble* thing to do than open your home and hearts to 3 lovely bro.-sister whose little hearts are longing for a mother & Father's love. I would understand that is Christian act. The very thought that they can be in the same home with same environments, the same future out-look. I'll write Mr. Wingate to let you take Dorothy on trial, until I can come to Trenton & take the matter up with you. I'll be in no hurry to come to Trenton. You have our most earnest prayers for you and the childrens success.

> Most Sincerely
> Mr. & Mrs. J. W. Swan

February 23, 1931—Woodruffs to Mr. Swan:

Dear Mr. Swan

We received your letter, Mr. Wingate asked us to take Dorothy for awhile in order that he might write his wife that Dorothy had been taken away—in an effort to get his wife back, he felt perhaps the jolt might bring her to her senses.

I never saw anyone more devoted to a child, and more interested. He asked that [she] be allowed to go to her own school over near his store. Of course, we were glad to do this for him, and know it will meet with your approval; also we can kill two birds with one stone. We can try Dorothy—. . .calls Mr. Woodruff 'daddy' although did not intend she should inasmuch if Mr. Wingate is able to take her back, and it might be hard to draw her away from us, and especially away from the children. She surely does enjoy her sister, Phyllis and Scottie. It is certainly a pleasure to have her and I am really in hope in many ways that everything works out so we can keep her although I feel that Wingates have first thought if he can arrange it. I am sure he will give her a good education and give everything possible for her.

Dorothy is such an attractive child and seems to mind nicely so far. I have no trouble with her at all.

With best wishes, we remain

Yours respectfully,
WOODRUFF & WOODRUFF
By ....

March 12, 1931—Mrs. Woodruff to Mr. Swan:

We received your letter a few days ago in regard to Dorothy. I believe that Mr. Wingate realizes that Mrs. Wingate will not return to him, as he stated he had a letter in which she refused to return— Mr. Wingate saying she was as mad as ever.

We still have Dorothy and as yet have not made up our minds as to whether we can keep her. She undoubtedly is a lovely child and very obedient, and gets along nicely with the children.

In this letter also it is revealed for the first time that Dorothy is suffering from some sort of dermatological condition:

When Dorothy first came to us from Mr. Wingate about three weeks ago, I noticed a breaking out or infection on different parts of her body and on her right fingers, etc. It being rather slight, I paid no attention to it. A few days ago a large boil developed on her back lower hip. I called Mr. Wingate about it, and when he brought her from school yesterday, he informed me she had had an attack of itch and that this was a recurrence of same. Of course, he should have told us in the first place, as I regret very much that our children are exposed but have not developed it as yet. Mr. Wingate said he supposed that she was alright. He brought a treatment to be used which he obtained from his doctor, so Dorothy and Phyllis are being fumigated today. The doctor thinks it will be a matter of three or four days when Dorothy will be all right.

March 16, 1931—the Woodruffs write Mr. Swan that Dorothy's skin condition has cleared up and they have decided to keep her.

March 18, 1931—Mr. Swan to the Woodruffs:

Dear Friends,

Your letter of 16th inst. recd. Contents considered. Glad to learn that Dora's skin disease was nothing serious I was quite sure It was something local. I have written Mr. Wingate to turn Dora over to you. You would be responsible for her. Do not believe Mrs. W. will return to live with him. When you study carefully the dispositions of the 3 you will find them not similar in every thing. May have to deal differently with each in training them. Wishing you abundant success, may you both receive Wisdom from whom Wisdom is promised, 'If any man lack wisdom Let him ask Him who is all Wisdom. 'giveth to them liberally & upbradeth a not.'

Most Sincerely,
Mr-Mrs. J. W. Swan

P. S. At anytime we can assist you let us know

Sometime between March 18 and the end of October—the Woodruffs write to Mrs. R. G. Neal, the visitor for the Children's Aid Society:

Dear Mrs. Neal:

If you will remember when we first took Dorothy, you said to me in Mr. Wingate's store that of course Mr. Wingate would like to see Dorothy at times and I said it would be all right with me.

Dorothy has been on a terrible nervous strain, is unable to sleep at nights for hours and I have no idea the cause. Today, she came home from school after Mr. Wingate had seen her and gave her some candy, and she had a nervous collapse and was unable to go to school. She also stated she was nervous in school and that her stomach 'jumped',—jerked, I think she meant.

I quizzed her to see what the difficulty was. For a time, I thought perhaps she wasn't adjusted at school and perhaps some of the children teased her. She stated that it made her nervous every time after Mr. Wingate came to see her and that was the reason she couldn't go to sleep at night easily. I had also noticed that she would be dreamy and morose after his visits but didn't think so much about it.

So, I just thought I would take it up with you to talk with Mr. Wingate that I feel for the best interests of Dorothy that he should refrain from having anything more to do with her. As you can see, as long as he keeps, coming, he retains some of her affections and it makes it rather hard on her, as the old saying goes, one cannot serve two masters.

I sympathize with Mr. Wingate, but I really feel if I had to give up Billy, I should never see him again because it would naturally stir him up everytime.

We hope you folks will take this letter in the spirit it is written, as I would not take this step if I did not think it was to Dorothy's best interests.

With kindest regards, I remain

Yours truly,

Later, in an undated letter written apparently sometime after October 31, the Woodruffs to the Reverend Swan:

Mr. J. H. Swan,
504 East 10th,
Sedalia, Missouri

Dear Mr. Swan:

Have been intending writing you for sometime inasmuch as we received a letter from the Children's Aid Society on October 31 stating that the Methodist Home for Children, St. Louis, had recently taken over the supervision of their Missouri children and, as I understand from the letter, Miss Georgia Greenleaf, Box 323, Jefferson City, Missouri, was their Field Secretary now.

If this means that you are no longer our 'Grandpa' we want to say here and now we don't like it. In fact, we didn't like the job at all of telling the children but they were real sweet about it. When I told them that perhaps you would not call and see us for the Society, Billy said, 'well, anyway, he is still our Grandpa.'

We really do feel like we had lost some of our family. Everyone of us always enjoyed your visits so much and so often when we had something to eat which the children enjoyed, one would remark that we ought to save it till Grandpa came. So you see how it is here. We all have certainly enjoyed our association and pleasant relations with you and Mrs. Swan, and surely hope we shall have the pleasure of meeting you both again. Anytime you happen to be through here, don't fail to call on us. The children are all fine—enjoying a Thanksgiving vacation. Phyllis and Dorothy are both taking violin in the school here and are considered quite talented. Billy, of course, is still in kindergarten and thinks he should have a horn to blow. He has high aspirations of being a member of the band at sometime.

With best wishes to you both from all, we are

>Yours very truly,
>WOODRUFF & WOODRUFF,
>By ....

Billy insisted that I read over this letter for him, which I did and then he insists that I add for him 'Sweet Grandpa Swan.'

December 5, 1931—Mr. Swan to the Woodruffs:

Mr. and Mrs. Geo Woodruff
Trenton, MO

Dear Friends. We thank you very much for your kind letter. The 22nd October I passed my 80 milestone. Mrs. Swan and I resigned. Now I am a man of *leisure* good for nothing. We greatly appreciate the fact that we met you & tried to interest you in our dear children. You assumed a great responsibility in taking the 3 dear ones. We believe you have laid by some treasure in heaven & trust the *Jewels* will greatly reward you. Mrs. Swan sends her congratulations to you and the children. Tell Billy I [crossed out] we are still grandma and grandpa. If you come to Sedalia come see us.

>Most Sincerely
>Mr-Mrs. J. W. Swan

By 1932 the Woodruffs had started proceedings to adopt all three of the Weir children. They wrote to the Children's Aid Society about their plans and on September 8, 1932, received the following response:

> Mrs. George E. Woodruff
> 903½ Main Street
> Trenton, Missouri.
>
> My dear Mrs. Woodruff:
>
> I have just returned from my vacation and have your very nice letter about the children and personally I am delighted that you and Mr. Woodruff want to adopt them.
>
> In matters of adoption we have always made it necessary to have a formal recommendation from the local visitor before writing the papers and I am writing Miss Greenleaf today about it. I have asked her to let me hear from her before the end of the month and when I do so I will communicate with you again.
>
> I have thought so many times of my visit to you and what a very happy family you all were. The children seemed like very promising little tots to me and very sweet ones too, so that I can understand how you are so devoted to them.
>
> > Yours sincerely,
> > (Miss) Helen Baxter
> > Supervisor of Free Homes.
>
> HB:ew

Miss Greenleaf's letter of recommendation must have arrived in New York very quickly, as the Woodruffs received a second letter from Helen Baxter only fifteen days after her first one. In this one she announces that the adoption papers are already drawn up.

> September 23, 1932.
>
> Mrs. George E. Woodruff,
> 903½ Main Street
> Trenton, Mo.
>
> My dear Mrs. Woodruff:
>
> We have the papers all prepared for the adoption of your three children and are sending them to you, under separate cover, by registered mail. I hope very much you will find them in proper order and that you will have no difficulty getting the proceedings through.
>
> We are also enclosing some Certificates of Adoption which we would be glad to have returned to the office when the adoptions are completed.

With best wishes to you and Mr. Woodruff, I am

Yours very truly,
Helen Baxter
Supervisor of Free Homes

HB:T

Despite Miss Baxter's speedy reply, the legal papers did not arrive in time to be filed in the November session of the Grundy County Court. However, they were ready for the session of February 1933.

March 6, 1933—the Woodruffs to a Miss Gilson of the Society:

The Children's Aid Society,
105 East 22nd Street,
New York.

Dear Miss Gilson:

This will acknowledge receipt of your letter of the 2nd, in which you inquire as to adoption proceedings and also whether we received the adoption papers.

We beg your pardon for not acknowledging receipt of same which you sent to us on September 23rd, 1932, but which did not arrive in time for us to prepare the necessary papers for the November term of Court.

However, same is on the present February Term of court and order of publication has been obtained, and the decree will be granted most anytime now—in other words, just as soon as it is called up. I notice it is the last case on the docket.

We shall be glad to return to you the certificates of adoptions which were also enclosed for our convenience.

The children are getting along so nicely—I wonder sometimes if there are any children just as lovely as they are—even the little 'flat nose' one is the pride of our heart and so happy. She so frequently asks me if there is anyone who is as happy as she. Both the girls are taking violin in the schools and our boy is in the first grade, attending only one-half day. They made satisfactory grades, a number of S and some E's, and enjoy their school work so much, needing no urging to go each day.

Thanking you for your inquiry and with kindest regards, we are

Yours very truly,
WOODRUFF & WOODRUFF
By ....

Thus, through the concern of two caring people and the workers of the Children's Aid Society, we leave the three children happily established in a permanent home.

There is an epilogue to this story, also on a happy note. It seems the Weir children had an older brother, Eddie, who had not been sent west on an orphan train, but had been taken by his father to Canada. Long after, when all the children were grown, Eddie traced his younger siblings to the town of Mexico, Missouri, in Audrain County, where they had moved with their adoptive parents. Thirty-two years after their separation, Eddie came to Mexico to visit, and the four Weirs were at last reunited. From Eddie, the others learned that their mother had died in 1928. After the three younger children had been placed with the Children's Aid Society, the father moved to Canada. Eddie had grown up there, reared by his grandparents, Mr. and Mrs. Ephram Rabideau, in Glenelm, Quebec.

But he never forgot his brother and sisters. Three of his children were named for them—Bill, Dorothy and Phyllis.

6: Financing the Orphan Trains

IN THE BEGINNING, when the plan for transporting orphans was devised, the Children's Aid Society had next to nothing for carrying out the plan. As Miriam Langsam wrote, "When first organized, the Society had no property, no promises of support, no appropriations, and no funds of any kind. Friends of the Society claimed that in its first year its only property was an ink bottle and some pens."[1]

It was Brace's early hope that the railroads would provide reduced rates or even free passage for the children. He was quickly disillusioned of that. Apparently, the cheapest transportation the railroads could offer was the emigrant trains—the dirty, smoky, crowded boxcars, such as the one which carried the first load of children to Michigan in 1854. But Brace was adamant, insisting on "decent style" for his orphans. Since neither the railroads nor the farmers and small town citizens of the Midwest and South would or could pay for such transportation, the Society was obliged to come up with the necessary funds.

One of the great arguments for transporting orphans was that it could be done inexpensively. The figure most often given was fifteen dollars per child, covering the cost of the ticket, food, clothing and lodging on the trip. Although, per child, this was a modest figure, there were many children. And raising the money proved more difficult than Brace and his board of directors had realized it would be. One of their first efforts at fund raising was a benefit concert in 1855. It was a fiasco.

> Our effort at musical benevolence became a series of most inharmonius squabbles. The leading soprano had a quarrel with the bass; the instrumental split with the vocal performers; our best solo went off in a huff, and, at last, by superhuman exertions we reconciled the dis-

cordant elements. . .and retired with a few hundred dollars.[2]

Unwilling to deal further with the temperaments of performers, Brace determined never again to resort to such methods. Nor would he use raffles or fairs to raise money, and he refused flatly to exploit children for the purpose. Even though many advisers and members of the board urged him to do so, Brace could not morally allow the exhibition of street children or anything which smacked of sensationalism.

There was another problem: In appealing to the wealthy for funds, the Society appeared to attack the very system that had made them wealthy. Many of those shrewd nineteenth century capitalists had profited from the use of cheap abundant immigrant labor. The Society's stated objective—to abolish or at least decrease juvenile delinquency in the cities—appeared to industrialists and businessmen as a threat to their labor supply.

There was no way of raising money which Brace found compatible with his nature. "No such disagreeable and self-denying work is ever done as begging money. The feeling that you are boring others, and getting from their personal regard, what ought to be given solely for public motives, and the certainty that others will apply to them, and expect a subscription as a personal return, are all great 'crosses'"[3]

However, the Reverend Brace was as practical as any capitalist and seemed to have been a born propagandist. He shouldered his cross and despite his distaste for the task proved to be very good at raising money.

One of his methods was somewhat at variance with his counsel that no charitable organization should be associated in the public mind with any specific group.

One rock, which the manager of such a movement must always steer clear of, is the sectarian difficulty. He must ignore sects, and rest his enterprise on the broadest and simplest principles of morality and religion. The animating force must be religious, especially the 'enthusiasms of humanity' shown in the love of Christ and for all who bear His image. But dogmatic teaching, and disputations, and sectarian ambitions, are to be carefully eschewed and avoided in such efforts of humanity. The public must learn gradually to associate the movement, not with any particular sect or church, but with the feeling of humanity and religion—the very spirit of Christ himself.[4]

The Quakers had historically worked for social welfare, particularly in regard to children. The Universalists and Unitarians, known since their merger as the Unitarian-Universalist Association, had a very liberal view of religious involvement in social welfare. Whether influenced by their practices or not, Brace went somewhat against his own dictum and turned to the churches, urging Christian cooperation in his cause.

As a minister he established contact with every Protestant church in the city. He made direct appeals to the Sunday schools to involve the children in giving money for the work of the Society. "What more cheering and encouraging sight than to see the children. . .saving a few cents for a weekly or monthly collection, in aid of neglected or destitute boys and girls," he wrote in the *First Annual Report of the Children's Aid Society.*

He soon found that he could and did spend six nights a week and all day Sunday speaking on behalf of the Society in most of the eastern cities. He never asked directly for contributions. He merely presented the case for the trains and "[left] the matter before the people for consideration."[5]

Disinclined as he was toward fund raising, he found to his surprise that he enjoyed the public meetings. "Evidently," he wrote with some pride, "to many minds, the fact that a man of education was dedicated to such pursuits was in itself an enigma or an eccentricity."[6] He was further surprised to find that not only city churches but those in rural areas supported the cause. One of the main arguments for the orphan trains was that they would help reduce juvenile problems in urban areas. But Brace observed that "some of our best bequests [have] come from the country." The largest contributions did, however, come from upper-class New York churches, chiefly Presbyterian and Congregational. But almost every Protestant denomination, including Baptist, Dutch Reformed, Unitarian, Methodist, Universalist, and a variety of independent churches, responded to these appeals.

(It was with some reason that most New Yorkers, especially the Catholics, considered the Children's Aid Society a

Protestant organization. In a sense it was. But it must be noted that when the Society was formed in 1853 not all the trustees belonged to the mainstream of Protestantism. Three of the seven were Unitarian: William C. Russell, the nephew of the noted Unitarian minister, William Ellery Channing; B. J. Howland, a friend of Russell's, whom Brace described as a man of "peculiar compassion of nature, whose life consisted of the happiness it shed on others;" and J. W. Williams, who served as treasurer until his death twenty-four years later.)

Though church donations were a dependable source of income, they provided only a fraction of the amount needed. Having developed personal contacts with newsmen early in his life, Brace now began to write to the papers, calling attention to the pathetic condition of the street children and emphasizing the successes of the Society. Unabashed, he sent in article after article. Writing to raise money, he noted, was an incessant activity. Nevertheless, he found that composing the news stories was a satisfying endeavor, as was his daily editing of the Society's publications.

Public money came slowly. "Year after year our application [for city or state funds] was rejected," Brace wrote. More and more then, as the trains became a major policy of the Society, he turned to individuals for financial support. He realized that favorable publicity, such as he was getting from the newspapers, would attract to the Society board wealthy men and women with a sense of *noblesse oblige*. Starting with the first significant donation—$15,000 from J. B. Barnard in 1856—the Society soon began acquiring money, property and services from volunteers. Brace had shrewdly realized that personal appeals to the wives and daughters of these upper-class gentlemen could be most effective. Persuaded by their women, many husbands and fathers made annual contributions. The women themselves worked with the Society as unpaid teachers, home visitors, letter writers, clerks and administrators. Some also volunteered to solicit funds, door-to-door, in the wealthier sections of the city.

One of the ladies who helped finance the placing-out policy was Mrs. John Jacob Astor. The Astor family had been substantial contributors from the beginning, especially to the building fund. In fact, John Jacob Astor himself was one of the earliest donors with his gift of fifty dollars in 1854. By 1871 Mrs. Astor had given the Society more than a thousand dollars. M. Bayard Brown and the Christian Union also had contributed a thousand dollars each,

That year Mrs. Astor donated forty-seven percent of the total amount of money from private individuals. In 1875 she contributed enough to send fifty boys west. In the next two years her annual gift of $1,500 sent a hundred boys. In addition, she sent out fifty more in 1878 to celebrate her son's wedding. By 1887 she was paying for the emigration of two hundred children annually. On her death the following year she left $25,000 to the Society for the emigration policy.

Altogether, Mrs. Astor's efforts accounted for the placement of approximately twelve hundred children. Though this was only about one percent of the total from 1855-1888, the publicity surrounding her contributions was invaluable to the Society's fund raising efforts. The New York papers regularly ran stories on the groups she sent out each year. Because of this publicity small and large donors alike helped to keep the trains running. Others, such as the Livingstons, the Sloans, the Vanderbilts, the Stuarts, the Fabbris and the Masons, saw their contributions as an obligation of the *nouveau riche*. That they helped control juvenile delinquency was an added incentive.

At the same time the Society was making poignant appeals to less wealthy New Yorkers, especially at Christmastime. Brace wrote special circulars urging children to encourage their parents to contribute.

> You are having a very happy time of CHRISTMAS day . . .As you warm yourselves at the blazing fire think of the cold and shivering little children of the great city wandering about the streets barefooted and half-clothed, hungry, downhearted, with no friends and no home. It will make a happier Christmas for you if you have given a home to a homeless boy.[7]

In the conclusion to his autobiography Brace wrote, "Of the modes in which money should be raised, I have already spoken. In all these matters, the general rule of wisdom is to avoid sensation; and to trust to the settled and reasonable conviction of the public, rather than to temporary feeling or excitement."[8] While rejecting the sensational, he was constant in his praise of capitalism as a moral virtue and free enterprise as a major instrument for the solving of social problems. Analyzing the success of the Society's fund raising efforts, he named as primary reasons the principles of self-help and work. These he considered part "of natural and economic laws," like class structure and the family. Children needed families, he believed, to teach them to work and not be revolutionaries. "The Industrial Schools [of the Society]. . .are seminaries of industry and teachers of order and self-help."[9]

Another reason for the success was the Society's workers' responsibility in financial matters. "A strict system of accountability has been maintained, step by step, from the lowest to the highest executive officer. Of many engaged in the labors of the Association, it can be truly said, that no business or commercial house was ever more faithfully and earnestly served, than this charity has been by them."[10] In a nineteenth century industrial society no higher praise could be given to a charity enterprise than to report its financial stability.

Brace portrayed the members of the board as businessmen who through their sense of management could accomplish anything. "Two or three men of their position, wealth, and ability, who should take the moral interest of any class of our population on their hands, and be in earnest in the thing, could not fail to accomplish great results."[11]

Under the guidance of businessmen the Society turned more and more to interest bearing accounts. The largest of these was the Rose Fund, established by Chauncey Rose, the railroad magnate. His brother John had died, leaving the Society $900,000 in his will. Because of its vague wording, Chauncey had the will set aside. However, he felt that the work of the Society was sufficiently important that he established the Rose Fund, with the stipulation that only the interest from it could be used for the transportation policy. It was his belief that deportation of street children was the best solution to many of the city's problems, and before he died he contributed over $200,000 in his own name and his brother's for the orphan trains.

Turned down in earlier years, the Society began in time to receive grants from state, county and local governments. In 1871 the New York Board of Education contributed $11,000 for the operation of the industrial schools. An additional $50,000 in unrestricted funds came from the city and county governments.

Though Brace did not think it politically wise to use this money for the orphan trains, its availability released other money for the purpose. Miriam Langsam believes that perhaps as much as $12,000 a year was diverted from governmental sources to support the transportation policy. But her conclusion is based on the surpluses the Society had from operating the industrial schools. It is her assumption that these surpluses probably went toward other operations, such as employees' salaries, and only incidentally for the costs of the trains.

In 1874 one of the criticisms of the Society from both the New York State Legislature and the *Catholic World* was that the salaries of the superintendent, the visitors, the agents and the teachers were inordinately high. The *Catholic World* reported that the Society spent only one-fourth of its budget on children, while most of the money went to the officers. "At all events," the editors wrote, "in the present instance it is clear that the [Society's] schools are less intended to instruct the children than to support the teachers."[12]

Periodic investigations by state and city officials never produced any evidence of the Society's misuse of funds. Because of the careful record keeping by the treasurer, J. W. Williams, the board could open its books at any time to public or governmental bodies. In its investigaton in 1871 the Committee on Charities of the Senate of New York found that not a dollar had been misappropriated or squandered. The committee did not consider the question raised by the *Catholic World* of overpaying Society employees, even though Brace admitted that the board had always treated them liberally. But, he wrote, "Not a single employe, so far as he is aware, in all this time, during his service has ever wronged the Society or betrayed its trust."[13]

As for Williams, Brace so admired the man that in the addenda to *The Dangerous Classes* he devoted an entire section to him. Williams' work, he noted, went far beyond his duties as treasurer. "He visited the Schools and Lodging Houses, watched the Emigration parties, studied carefully the accounts and reports of the different agents, and knew the multifarious work of the Society thoroughly. His especial interest was the Emigration parties, and for this he procured important assistance."[14] (Much of this assistance came in the form of contributions from influential business people who were Williams' personal friends.)

By the time of Williams' death the Children's Aid Society had spent more than a million dollars, had an annual income of $175,000, owned several buildings in New York City and was completely free of debt.

For an organization starting out with a few pens and a bottle of ink, this was remarkable growth. The Reverend Brace and many others had labored diligently—speaking, writing, seeking support from institutions and individuals. It was typical of Brace that he credits the success of their financial growth to non-sectarian Christian business people, who operated under the principles of capitalism and free enterprise to bring about public good.

Notes to Chapter 6

1. Miriam Z. Langsam, *Children West*, p. 33.
2. Brace, *The Dangerous Classes of New York*, pp. 280-281.
3. Langsam, p. 33.
4. Brace, p. 446.
5. Brace, p. 281.
6. *ibid.*
7. Langsam, p. 33.
8. Brace, p. 417.
9. Brace, p. 442.
10. *ibid.*
11. Brace, pp. 444-445.
12. Langsam, p. 44.
13. Brace, p. 443.
14. Brace, p. 453.

7: An End and a Beginning

IN WAYS BOTH SUBTLE and direct, the success of the trains had a considerable effect on the country's attitude toward orphans. In some midwestern areas there were those, of course, who frowned on the policy. Forgetting that they too were of immigrant stock, they were suspicious of those racially, culturally and socially unidentified children dropped into their midst.

There were many more, however, who learned quickly to appreciate the children, to respect the hardships they had endured so pluckily. It was not only the need for extra workhands but genuine compassion that led so many farmers, small town families and whole communities to open their hearts and homes to so many young waifs.

On all those whose lives were directly touched by the orphans they became a shaping influence. As Gladys Lawyer said of her husband Alclo and his brothers, all of whom came on an orphan train, "They were, and are, my very life."

In Lebanon, Missouri, we found that the townspeople still take pride in having been a part of that humanitarian endeavor. Local lore of the trains dates back at least eighty years. On June 7, 1910, the Lebanon *Republic* reported on the front page:

> The local committee, composed of Sam R. Farrar, Dr. J. M. Billings, J. W. Farris, W. I. Wallace, and E. B. Kellerman, and J. G. Lingeweiller, had received about seventy-five applications for children, hence there was no difficulty in securing satisfactory homes for the twelve brought here.
>
> The children were exceptionally bright and attractive, ranging in age from 2½ years to 15 years.

There are residents in Lebanon today who still have memories of the trains and the orphans who found homes in their

Miss Anne Hill and B. W. Tice, with children brought to Lebanon, Missouri, January 1910. Group includes four Rifenburgh children.

town. Lois Roper Beard writes of them in her *History of Laclede County.*

> The trip to Missouri on the train was a long one, which left memories. With four other children of the home, Miss Hill and Mr. Tice the Superintendent crossed the river by ferry to be met by the children from an orphanage from New Jersey. . .The children ate sandwiches and apples and slept in their seats never leaving the train all the way. They were taken to the opera house on reaching Lebanon. There Mr. Tice made a talk on the care of them and requirements and instructions.[1]

She also tells of a little girl named Jennie, who arrived

in Lebanon with her brother Harry on January 29, 1910. That day, Joe and Belle Holman had come to inspect the orphans, and the moment he laid eyes on Jennie, Joe Holman said, "That's my little girl." Though she and her brother were placed in separate homes, Jennie seems to have had a happy life with her new family.

Wherever the young riders landed they made some impact, even on those who, like Harry E. Newland, of Chanute, Kansas, had little direct contact with them. He writes:

> In regard to the Orphan train which came to Chanute, Kansas, after the first World War I can only relate the apparent facts which I heard during my first forty years years as a resident of Chanute.
> I worked several years on the Santa Fe railroad with a man named George Riker who said he and his sister were on the 'Train.' I do not know the identity of the sister other than the fact that she was married and lived on a farm. George has since retired and I believe died several years ago in Arizona. His son George Jr. in 1983 lived at 1217 W. 14th Court in Chanute.
> The author of the well known song 'Nature Boy' and his sister were on the train and they were adopted by a druggist, Mel McGrew. 'George McGrew' later changed his name back to his family name, Eben Ahbez, and last lived in California.[2]

One wonders how much personal experience went into that song about a "strange enchanted boy," who wrote of love as the "greatest thing you'll ever learn. . ."

Harry Newland also remembers a brother and sister, John and Mary Belle Nation, who were taken into the home of C. S. Nation, a Chanute businessman. They were very popular in school, he recalls.

Mrs. Eva Lloyd of Maryville, Missouri, interviewed in June 1986 by Evelyn Trickel, has pleasant memories of her friend and foster cousin Flossie. At the age of ten Flossie arrived on an orphan train in Gallatin, Missouri, in Davies County, and was placed with Eva's aunt and uncle, the Gustavisons. "Seemingly she was adjusted in the family quite well." Although Flossie was never legally adopted, she "called her parents, as I recall, Mama and Papa, and she was part of the family." Probably because she remembered them very dimly, Flossie never spoke of her natural parents or the train experience. To young Eva this gave her new cousin an added dash of mystery. Today Florence Gustavison lives in California, but maintains a close relationship with members of her foster family. Almost sixty years after the last train stopped in Missouri, Eva Lloyd concludes in retrospect,

> Perhaps we would be amazed for anyone to be chosen within a few hours or few minutes. So I believe, without knowing all the facts, it seems to me, that the orphan train served a wonderful purpose for some of these who had good experiences. This experience with Flossie has always stayed in my mind as a very good and appropriate use of the orphan trains.

Although this sentiment is frequently echoed, Brace's plan, as we know, was not perfect. The Children's Aid Society had its failures as well as its successes. There were instances of incompatibility between children and foster parents. Occasionally the agents discovered child abuse and neglect, cases of overwork and malnourishment. The Society made every effort to investigate such cases and remove the child. (These home visits continued for years, even after the end of the trains. The case of the three Weir children is an example, continuing as it did into 1933.) But the agents had many children to look after and could visit only once or twice a year. There were bound to be oversights and occasionally children like Mary Goth, Marian Burke, and others, who suffered at the hands of foster parents.

Abuse and rejection did not often happen after a child was placed. In fact, some foster parents seem to have enjoyed their new child so much that they did what they could to help him adjust to a new environment. Such was the case of James Lewis McCarthy, who was placed with the Melton family in Sullivan County, Missouri. This farm life was a far cry from New York City, and the boy grew so homesick that the Meltons sent for his sister and made her a part of the family also. As we learn from James' daughter, Bonnie Council, interviewed by Evelyn Trickel in June 1986, the Meltons did not feel financially able to take a third sibling, another boy. But James felt so much a part of the family that he went by the family name. Mrs. Council believes that the

Meltons were in the process of adopting him when Mr. Melton died.

No doubt there were other orphans who were mistreated and unhappy, whose stories we have not heard. But we have found few records of real bitterness. A common thread through most of their stories is gratitude for the orphan trains and a system which gave them a home and a family.

This is in marked contrast to a much later transportation of children, following World War II, when the British government shipped two thousand orphans to Australia. In two articles in *The Observer* (July 19 and 26, 1987), Sue Adler writes of English children embittered by the experience. Ms. Adler calls the separation of siblings "one particularly callous aspect of the migration scheme." She concludes that "The policy of exporting Britain's unwanted children to a continent 13,000 miles away will always remain a shameful chapter in Britain's social history."

Certainly, the separation of siblings was one of the least acceptable features of the placing-out system. Yet it did occur, along with the other practices which may seem harsh to us today: the disregard of racial and religious questions; uprooting children from familiar environment; and their removal from poverty stricken parents who may have wanted to keep them. Even if children were overworked by foster parents, as long as they were treated as family members, they were rarely removed.

Yet regardless of these shortcomings, the Reverend Brace had developed a system which seemed remarkably effective. It lasted for seventy-five years, and in that time the orphan trains had carried an estimated 150,000 children to new homes in the West and South. But it was not merely the number of orphans carried which made Brace's program so impressive, it was his constant emphasis on home and family and their importance to the children. (It is ironic that while advocating the importance of the family environment, he was allowing the separation of children from the only family they had ever known—their brothers and sisters. Still, brothers and sisters, young as most of them were, do not make a family, nor provide the security of a home with parental care and authority.)

Brace and the Society were the first to implement foster home placement to such an extent. Therein lay its singularity—and Brace's primary claim to success. Due in great part to his efforts, a change of attitude took place among those involved in child welfare. No longer did the traditional idea prevail that the orphanage was the only place for homeless children. Building more and more warehouses to store them in was not the answer. The orphan home system began to give way to the idea of family, and the "asylum party," as Brace called it, was put to rout.

By the turn of the century Brace's insistence on the importance of family gained broader and increasing acceptance. In 1909 President Theodore Roosevelt called the first White House Conference on Children. Here, however, the idea of family changed somewhat. The emphasis now fell not so much on the foster family as on the natural family. The conference was almost unanimous in recommending that biological families should be kept together. It was a logical progression from Brace's original concept, that one way or another, every child should be part of a family.

Building on previous programs, seeing that his own was carried out with integrity and compassion, what Charles Loring Brace had done within half a century was to revolutionize the approach to the treatment of orphans. It was the very success of his plan that brought it to an end. As further social reforms took place and the emphasis shifted to the natural rather than the foster family, there was less need for transporting children to homes in other parts of the country. The need for the trains therefore decreased. And in 1929 the last orphan train left New York City, bound for the Middlewest, thus bringing to a close a unique episode in the history of the United States.

It is a sad and alarming fact that the situation for children is as desperate today as it was when Brace first began his work. Estimates of the number of homeless people in America range from 200,000 to 600,000. According to Charles King writing in *The Humanist,* 1989, fifteen percent of the homeless are children under the age of five. In 1988 Jonathan Kozol, who has written frequently on the subject, suggested that half the homeless in New York were children with an average age of six.[3]

Tragic though these figures are, they do not diminish Brace's achievement in his time. In the preface to his book, *Boston's Wayward Children,* Peter Holloran writes that in popular and professional literature on child welfare there is agreement on one point at least: "that America fails to provide for the well-being of children and adolescents without adequate parents or guardians." This is precisely what Brace campaigned for throughout his career—adequate parents and homes for his orphans, a family situation. His concept is as valid today as it was then, and his real achievement lies in his commitment to it. His success in finding homes for thousands of children, who might otherwise have languished in orphanages or perished on the streets, is even today significant.

The commitment of so many Americans is also of lasting significance, particularly that of the families who took in the children sent west and south on the orphan trains. In her article on the removal of British orphans, Sue Adler quotes from a number of those who were sent to Australia. Shirley Ronge called it "the worst thing they ever did, sending me out there." And George Wilkins, who is now a millionaire, found it "a place totally without love." By contrast the American Midwest seems to have been a place of much love and much generosity of spirit.

It may be due in great part to the American character that the western immigration system worked as well as it did. It is part of the American mystique that, through tenacity and hard work, any individual, regardless of ancestry or environment, can achieve success. The lives of so many of these orphans, who became worthy citizens with strong family ties, are ample proof of that conviction. And in the end, the credit must be given to the children themselves, who fulfilled the Reverend Brace's vision, to the street arabs and the storehouse children—young, cast out, exiles through no fault of their own, but blessed with courage and determined to survive.

Notes to Chapter 7

1. Lois Roper Beard, *The History of Laclede County* (Tulsa, Okla.: The Heritage Publishing Co., 1979), pp. 110-111.

2. Harry E. Newland, letter to Michael Patrick, July 30, 1986.

3. Charles King, "Homelessness in America," *The Humanist* (May/June 1989), p. 8. Also see Jonathan Kozol, *Rachel and Her Children: Homeless Families in America* (New York: Crown Publishers, 1988), passim.

8: The Orphans' Stories

Personal history is often most eloquent and revealing when related by the person himself. We have been fortunate in hearing accounts of early experiences directly from some of those who came west as children on the orphan trains. There are not many of them left now, and their first-hand stories are to be treasured.

We are fortunate too in that so many family members and friends of the orphans have come forward with memories of the train riders. They have supplied us generously with memoirs and memorabilia, giving us vivid pictures of adventures and misadventures experienced by those children.

Throughout this history of the orphan trains, we have alluded to the many difficulties, physical and emotional, which faced the children. In the following stories you will find frequent mention of such problems and the ways they were endured and, happily, most often overcome.

Passages quoted from the narrators, like those in previous chapters, appear in their own words. The language, spelling and punctuation are their own.

DOROTHY AND SUSAN BOND

(From Susan Bond Schulz, letters to Evelyn Sheets, December 26, 1985, and January 8, 1986.)

When they were six years old, the twin sisters, Dorothy and Susan Bond, were placed in an orphanage in Brooklyn, New York. Many years later, in 1985, Susan Bond Schulz wrote of that period as the happiest in her life. "On every Saturday we went to the Brooklyn Bridge for a walk or to Coney Island. We then went home and had our usual meal, ginger snaps and milk. On Sundays we went to Trinity Church for services."

The life they found so blissful was to last a mere two years. When they were eight it was decided that the twins

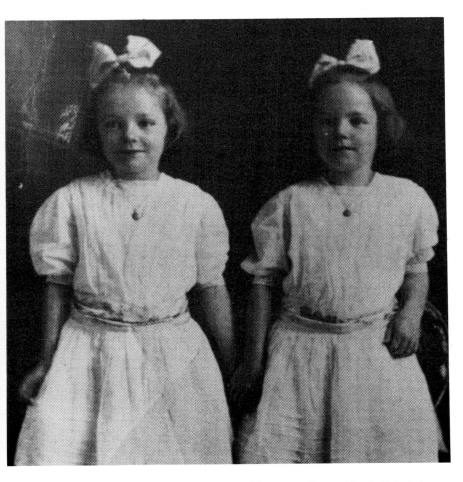

The Bond twins, Dorothy and Susan. *(Courtesy Susan Bond Schulz.)*

would be taken west on an orphan train. "The day we were to leave Mr. Swan of Sedalia, Missouri, came after us. We were checked by a doctor, given a bath, new clothes and both of us crying for we didn't want to leave. With Mr. Swan we went then to the train and cried all the way to Vandalia [Missouri]." As she remembers, five children got off there. "We were taken to the opera house and people just took us. They wanted to separate me and my sister but Mr. Swan would not allow [it]. . .Different people told me later that we both cried during the whole *show*."

The little girls were first taken by a Dr. and Mrs. Alford. "We lived only a short while with the Alfords as he said she was mean to us. I don't remember that." She is apparently referring to Mr. Swan, as he soon moved the girls to the home of Mr. and Mrs. McPike, with whom they lived for the next fourteen years, until 1924.

The years were not entirely happy. "I have no idea why our parents took us in for it was not a happy home. The McPike family never quite accepted us but our mother's family were wonderful people."

Nevertheless, the girls did have some good times. "We started our social life [in] 1920. There were eight of us and called our club J. F. F. (Just For Fun). We just hiked [and had] skating parties and when we got older we started playing bridge and still do."

Like most of the orphan train riders with whom we have been in contact, the Bond twins had many questions about their biological parents.

> We tried for years to find out something about our family but all the letters we wrote knew nothing about Lulu Bond. In July 10, 1924 we had a letter from the Brooklyn Saving Bank that they had two accounts in that bank deposited by Lulu Bond one in a trust for Susan Bond and one in trust for Dorothy Bond. There was a lot of correspond [sic] and finally in December 25, 1924 from the Aid Society that Mr. E. H. Opitz worked hard for the money and persuaded the bank to turn the money over to them. They enclosed a check for $36.44 for each of us. We wrote and thanked him for his trouble.

In 1924 Susan Bond was married to Carl Schulz. Their two sons died at birth. Perhaps if Susan had had genetic information about her real parents her children might have been saved.

Dorothy Bond died in 1972. Her sister wrote, "She and her husband, Smith Hagen, lived in Sun City, Arizona. I went out in December [1972] and stayed with her till she died. She had cancer but never complained so we enjoyed ourselves what time we were together."

Dorothy had one daughter, who now lives in California. She and her aunt keep in close touch with each other.

ESTHER HOLMAN BOWDISH

(From an article in the Des Moines Register, *1980.)*

Margaret Pierce Holman, the wife of a Baptist minister, died only two months after the birth of her daughter, Esther. The child was taken into the home of her mother's sister, who wanted to adopt her. But the sister was Catholic, and neither Esther's father nor her grandfather, who was also a Baptist minister, would agree to the adoption.

Two years later her father remarried and Esther was returned to him. Then her stepmother died, her father went into the service, and Esther lived with her grandparents until she was placed with the Children's Aid Society.

She remembers little about coming to Iowa. "But I remember way back, a faint recollection only, of sitting on luggage at a station in Manchester, where people from Earlville and all around came to meet the orphan train. We were taken to a theater with numbered placards hung about our necks. People looked us over, made first, second, third choices." At the theater, a man named Amzie Davey said to his wife, "I know which one I want. That little girl over there." When his wife asked why, Amzie replied, "She's just so busy with the other kids." With that, as the story goes, Esther put her hand in Maude Davey's and said, "Come on, mama, let's go home."

Thus, a little girl whose father was a Baptist, whose mother came of a Catholic family, became a Congregationalist, adopting the faith of her foster parents.

The agent from the Children's Aid Society visited Esther at the Daveys' home twice a year. On one of these trips the agent had two boys with her, whose placement had not been successful. One of the boys was blind in one eye. But Esther's foster grandfather, who lived across the street, asked if he could keep both boys. They were later adopted by Esther's foster aunt.

Even though her life with the Daveys was good, especially when they moved to a farm between Earlsville and Dyersville, Esther always wondered about her natural parents. Reassuring her, Maude Davey often told her during her childhood, "I wish I could have known your mother. She must have been a wonderful lady, because you are such a good girl." During World War II Esther tried to enlist in the military but was rejected for lack of a birth certificate.

In 1951, after her marriage to Don Bowdish, she and her husband went to New Jersey in search of her birth records. Having a clue that her parents had lived in Hackettstown, they stopped at a service station there and asked the operator if he had ever heard of Robert Holman. The man said he thought Robert Holman had been a ballplayer in town, but that his mother could probably give them more information. As they learned from his mother, Esther's parents had once lived next door and Esther was born in that house. "Two finer persons never put feet in shoes than your mother and father," the lady told her. For Esther that was "a lovely description. It was most satisfying to me."

The next day she received a message from her first cousin, who lived in a nearby town. "I am your closest living relative," the cousin said when they met. "I have never stopped praying for you. I wheeled you to the station when you left Hackettstown." That Sunday Esther went to the cemetery, where she found the graves of her mother, a brother and a sister.

Through her cousins she obtained a photograph of her mother, and from a historical feature in the Hackettstown newspaper she found a picture of her father, who had played on the best basketball team the town had ever had. Now that she had learned more of her ancestry, she felt she had two families, the Holmans and the Daveys.

ELIZABETH CONLIN

(Bessie Elizabeth Bartmess)

(From her daughter, Eunice Stroh Reeser, letters to Evelyn Sheets [handed on to Evelyn Trickel], and Michael Patrick, June 1987 and March 1988.)

On October 29, 1894, an unwed English Catholic woman named Lizzie Conlin gave birth to a daughter in Sloane Maternity Hospital in New York City. Barely two weeks later, the child, named Elizabeth, was placed in the Infant Asylum. Eight days later she was transferred to the Asylum's country branch in Mt. Vernon, New York. She remained there until May 28, 1900, when she was turned over to the Children's Aid Society and placed on an orphan train.

One of the train's destinations was Milan, Missouri. On the day it stopped there, Elza Bartmess had gone to the station to select an orphan. What she wanted was a dark-haired girl with curls. But when a red-haired, freckle-faced tomboy climbed into his lap and said, "Are you going to be my daddy?" he changed his mind on the spot.

At that time Elza and his wife Sadie lived in Boynton. Soon after they moved to a sod house on a farm in Woods County, Oklahoma. Then, in January 1904, the couple legally adopted the little girl and changed her name to Bessie Elizabeth Bartmess.

Sadie Bartmess, who was unable to have children of her own, died at the age of thirty-six of "a gathering in the head." She had two dying wishes—one, that her husband would marry her sister Bertha; the other, that he would take good care of Bessie. A year later Elza and Bertha were married. But in the intervening year, he and his adopted daughter had become quite close, close enough, it seems, that when Bertha was about to have her first child she delivered an ultimatum: Elza would have to choose between her and Bessie. Feeling that he could not abandon a pregnant woman, Elza asked Bessie to leave.

Elza's father was also living in the home at that time, and Bertha had apparently set her foot down about him, as well. According to family lore, the old man, not knowing where to go, just set off down the road with his suitcase. It was a hot day in July, and the old man died on the road of a heat stroke.

Banished from home, Bessie went to work in Alva, Oklahoma, as a domestic and attended school through the tenth grade. Twice, however, she was called home to help with the birth of stepsisters and take care of the woman who had turned her out.

Had her father permitted, Elizabeth, now Bessie, could have been married very early. One of her playmates in the New York orphanage was a boy named Roy Jenkins, who had been sent to Missouri earlier. On the day young Elizabeth arrived in Milan, he was waiting at the station to greet her.

Roy was seven years older than she. When he was twenty-one he asked Bessie to marry him. But since Bessie was only fourteen, Elza Bartmess forbade it.

After caring for Bertha during the birth of the second child, Bessie went back to work for a family in Alva. She was encouraged by that family to become a schoolteacher. After a brief try, she gave it up (partly because she was weak in mathematics), took a course in Pittman shorthand, and earned her living as a public stenographer. At one point she had a job in Wichita. Because her office had no typewriter, she had to write all the correspondence by hand. But occasionally she used a typewriter in the office across the hall, and it was there she met Louis Calvin Stroh, a man four years her junior. They were married on August 30, 1916, during their lunch hour.

For the next sixty-five years Bessie worked as a homemaker, raising two children, Arden and Eunice. Her husband took great pride in the fact that his wife never had to go outside the home to take a job. Having learned telegraphy at the age of seventeen, Louis Stroh was for a time employed by the railroad in Durant and in Wichita. Later he worked for brokerage firms in Emporia, Kansas, in Denver, and in Kansas City. He retired at seventy and died on December 8, 1981, at the age of eighty-three.

At this writing, Bessie Bartmess Stroh, born Elizabeth Conlin, is ninety-three and lives in a nursing home in Walnut Creek, California, near the home of her daughter, Eunice Reeser. She has four granddaughters and nine great-grandchildren.

ROSE AND FRANK CRANOR

(From Rose Cranor, interviewed by Evelyn Sheets, June 6, 1985, and Michael Patrick, September 1, 1985. Additional information from her daughter, Bedonna Rice.)

In 1930, thirteen years after he and his sister Rose had been placed in Missouri, Frank Cranor, who had become an artist, returned to New York City, his birthplace. There with the help of Miss Anne Hill, one of the agents of the Children's Aid Society, he began to seek information on his natural par-

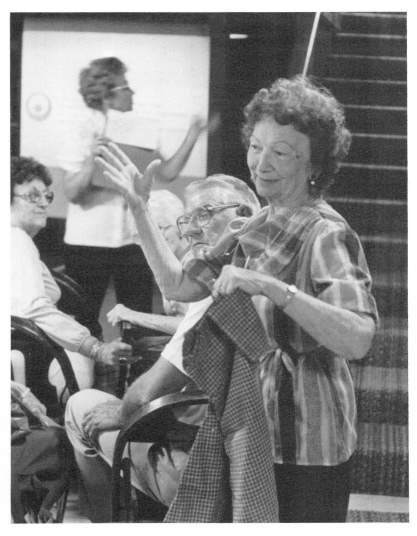

Reunion at Trenton, Missouri, 1985: Rose Cranor with the dress she wore on the orphan train. Lester Studer seated behind her. Evelyn Sheets in background, against white poster. *(Courtesy Evelyn Trickel.)*

ents. In 1942 he finally located his father. Frank's sister Rose gave us some of her recollections.

My father said I was born on the Brooklyn Bridge. That's when I first learned my true birth date, May 27,

1912. My mother was Catholic and my father Protestant. We were German and I spoke German. My mother supposedly deserted me two weeks after I was born. Our father took care of my brother and me for about four years before placing us in an orphanage.

During the four years with their father, his work had forced him to leave the two young children for long hours with the landlady of the tenement where they lived. Realizing that he could not care for them properly, he gave them up.

I remember my father. He was very good to us. He was a chauffeur, wore a uniform and he was friends of Charlie Chaplin. I remember meeting [Chaplin]. Later we were placed in the Children's Aid Society Home. My brother and I remember playing outside there and seeing our father standing by a tree and watching us play. We saw him crying.

Shortly after, in the late summer or fall of 1916, Rose and Frank joined other children on an orphan train. Frank was then seven years old, Rose only four. It was Miss Anne Hill who chaperoned them on the trip west.

In the course of the journey Rose fell and broke a leg and had to be hospitalized. The journey was evidently delayed, but eventually Frank was sent on with fourteen other orphans and arrived in Albany, Missouri, Gentry County, in February 1917. He became a member of the Swetnam family. On March 11 his little sister Rose reached Albany and was placed with Mr. and Mrs. William Whitton.

I was brought to what used to be the Merchants Hotel here in Albany. I remember being at the hotel. There were fourteen other children with my brother, who came a month earlier, but I was alone when I came. My brother and I were both adopted here in Albany but in different families. I already had been spoken for when I came. Mr. Swan of the Children's Aid Society came once a year after that to interview us to see if we were well taken care of and happy in our new homes.

Although she was separated from her father and to some extent from her brother, Rose had no regrets. She believed that her father was a "kind, good man" who loved his children so much that he gave them up to provide them with a better life. Still, she was somewhat haunted by the past and how her life might have turned out.

Yes, I am glad that I came to Albany. I had a happy life with good foster parents, and a foster sister. Yet, I have wondered what my life would have been had I stayed in New York with my parents. I would have had a completely different life. I have thought it strange how fate sets you up. And whatever fate gives you, that is what you've got.

Rose Cranor died in the fall of 1985 at the age of seventy-three. Her brother Frank died in 1980.

GERALD DOTY

(From his foster sister, Kathleen Moats, letter to Evelyn Sheets, March 11, 1985.)

On April 11, 1929, one of the last of the orphan trains arrived in Trenton, Missouri, the children accompanied by the Society agents, the Reverend and Mrs. J. W. Swan. Two items in the Trenton *Republican-Times* carry the story. The first, on April 11, announces the arrival of the train (mistakenly referring to J. W. Swan as J. T. and omitting mention of Mrs. Swan).

Swan is Here with Nine More Orphans
Only 7 of them Are to be Placed Near Here;
All Are Boys and Farm Homes Preferred.

J. T. Swan arrived in Trenton this morning, right on schedule, bringing a total of nine boys here, seven of whom he hopes to place with farmers of the vicinity. Two of the boys already have been found homes, one in Henry County and the other in Nebraska.

The boys are aged 6 to 14 years. While some of them will probably be placed in city homes, the farms have the first choice, Mr. Swan said, believing that all in all the environment is better for them there.

There are two boys who are brothers to some of the girls brought here on the last trip. One of these is fourteen years old and is a brother of the girl taken by Mr. and Mrs. J. W. Reynolds. The boy is a good student,

Mr. Swan said, [has a] year of high school, whom Mr. Swan would like to place in a home, close to town, where he can complete his education. The boy is a good student, Mr. Swan said, and otherwise recommends him strongly.

Another boy, 8 years old, is a brother of the girl taken by Mr. and Mrs. G. W. Alley. A third boy is one who has a brother at Green City, and Mr. Swan said he would like to place this boy in that section of the county, where they would not be far apart.

He will headquarter at the Trenton Hotel while here, and expects to be here a week or perhaps more, while he is finding homes for this group of children.

As the second story on April 17 reveals, it took only six days for the Swans to complete their task. All the boys were placed with families in or near Trenton. (The story, which also mentions three girls brought on the previous trip, appears in full in Chapter Five, in the account of the Weir children.) Although the article of April 11 stated that the boys were "aged 6 to 14," one of them, Gerald Doty, was only five. From his foster sister, Kathleen Fear Moats, we have this story of his placement. As she recalls, her parents had also taken a girl. Whether at the same time or earlier, she doesn't say, only that the Fears "took Gerald and a girl to live with them but couldn't seem to manage the girl. . .She was taken back to Trenton, and Gerald remained with them."

The little boy had liked it well enough to stay. He and Kathleen attended the first eight grades at the school in Tindall. After graduation from high school, Gerald joined the navy and served in World War II. He was recalled to duty during the Korean war.

It was not until he was in the navy that the Fears decided to adopt Gerald. Papers were drawn up by a lawyer in Princeton, Missouri, and sent to Gerald to be signed. By this time he had been discharged from the navy and was working at the Sunflower ordinance plant. Kathleen Moats and her parents were then living in DeSoto, Kansas, and the three of them went to Princeton with Gerald for his adoption procedure.

The adoption was typical of that of many of the orphan train riders. Often, if the parents did decide to adopt the child, it took place many years later.

ALEXANDER COLOWSKY DOUTHIT

(From interviews with Evelyn Trickel, June 2, 1986, and Michael Patrick, July 15, 1987.)

As Alexander Douthit discovered many years later, his mother died in the flu epidemic of 1918. His father was killed by accident or was murdered. That is all he knows of them. His earliest memories are of "a bunch of kids living together in a home—a regular home, not an orphanage."

Whether it was his home or another, Alexander does not recall, for he was very young when "this man" took him and his nine-month-old brother to a building downtown. The man told the lady at the desk that he would come back for them. He never did. The next day the boys were loaded on a bus and taken to an orphanage. There were "lots of kids and the people were very strict," Alexander says, and he was scared, particularly of the dark. Later they allowed him to sleep near a lantern in the hallway.

When he was about six years old, he and his baby brother were placed on an orphan train. The children were given sandwiches out of boxes in a back room of the station. The train stopped in Clarinda, Iowa, where they stayed at the Leatherton Hotel until their chaperones took them to the Methodist church, two blocks away. In the church the children walked up an down the aisles so that the crowd could see and talk to them. Alexander's brother was taken by Roy Davis, Alexander by a family named Baker. He had been with the family only three months, when Mrs. Baker became pregnant and the boy was moved into the Applequist home. The Applequists kept "a lot of kids," Alexander recalls, adding that they were very kind and never said a harsh word to any of them.

Because the Applequists felt they could not afford to keep him, Alexander was then moved to a third home, that of Harry Quentin Douthit and his wife Florence Josephine. Though he was moved three times within a year, he was never over twenty miles away from his little brother. But even that distance was not easily covered in those days and because of that and constant farm work, the brothers rarely saw each other.

Alexander's foster mother was kind, protective and generous. His foster father was a strict, hard-working man with a quick temper, who often resorted to physical punishment. But one of Alexander's happiest memories was his ninth birthday, when his father bought him a present. Alexander had never been given a birthday present before, and he laughed out loud with pleasure. On his eleventh birthday he received another—a low wheel cultivator! It was a gift typical of his father, something that would help the boy get more work done on the farm.

His father was the kind of man "who wouldn't apologize to the Good Lord," Alexander says. Once, when Mrs. Douthit wanted her husband to buy a box of chicken feed, he said, "That's foolish. Feed them oats and corn." For three days she gave him "a cold, silent shoulder." On the third day, her husband brought home a box "big enough to feed 10,000 chickens for five years, slammed it on the porch, and never said another word." As they sat down to supper that night, Mrs. Douthit picked up a plate and said, "Want some potatoes, Dad?" and that was the end of the matter.

Alexander was legally adopted by the Douthits on June 30, 1922. His parents never brought up the fact that he was an adopted child. His father, he says, never referred to it "even when he was mad. . ." And in the community Alexander experienced no prejudice, even though everyone knew he had been an orphan. To the other children he was just another kid, accepted in spite of his distinctive eastern dialect.

Alex grew up with the Douthits and graduated as valedictorian of his class. Although his father never approved of extracurricular activities (feeling that school was a place for study, not play, and Alexander should be home doing chores), Alex was a successful high school athlete and a musician. He married his high school sweetheart, raised a family and retired with his wife to northern Missouri.

Looking back over his early years, Alexander Colowsky Douthit praises the orphan trains as "the most wonderful thing that ever happened because they provided homes, food and affection when you really didn't expect any affection."

There was an incident many years ago that still lingers in his mind. Some sixteen years after his adoption by the Douthits, he was driving down the road near the farm one day when he stopped to help a man with a flat tire. In the course of their conversation, he learned that the man's name was Baker and that he had a wife and one daughter. Alex realized at once that this might well be the Bakers, his first foster family, who had kept him only three months. Not wanting to open old wounds, he did not ask. The insecurity and many displacements of those early years were something a child would not easily forget, even long years afterward.

JAMES DOYLE

(From his daughter, Mary E. Turek, letter to Evelyn Sheets, October 14, 1985.)

In 1907 or 1908—the year is uncertain—James Doyle arrived in Princeton, Missouri, Mercer County, on an orphan train and was taken into the home of the Powell family. Knowing nothing of the child's background, Mrs. Powell sent a letter of inquiry to New York, asking about James and his biological parents. In November 1908, she received a letter from James' mother, saying that she and her two children had been separated by accident. Rachel Doyle explained how "this horrible thing happened."

She had lived with the children's father for almost fourteen years in poverty, often with nothing to feed her family but potatoes and milk gravy. Once she stole a ten-pound bag of flour to keep them from starving. When she could no longer bear for them to live in these conditions, she left her husband and moved to Cobblesville, New York. There she worked in a hotel for $2.50 a week, spending two dollars a week for someone to care for the children. From time to time people in the hotel gave her things for her little Dora and Zimmie, as she called the boy. She continued the work at the hotel until she fell ill.

For the next three months a black woman took them in. When she had recovered from the illness, Rachel worked for a time as a housekeeper for a priest. She later found work in the home of a man without a wife, who offered to give her and the children a home. They were not "legally married," she wrote, "only sworn together," and the man provided them with a home and good food.

Zimmie and his sister Dora were attending a Lutheran Sunday School, when some of the church women convinced

Dora that she should go to school in the new Lutheran home in New York City. Dora wanted to go, and her mother agreed. But Zimmie cried and didn't want to be separated from his sister. His mother then decided that both of them could go to New York, with the understanding that she could visit them whenever she wished.

As she saw them off at the train station, she did not realize that she would never see them again. Until she received the letter from Zimmie's foster mother, she had no knowledge of what happened to either child.

Rachel Doyle closed the letter, saying that she was lonely and sorrowful, but did not have the money to go to Missouri to see her son. She apparently accepted that he was better off with the Powells, and the boy remained with them.

James Doyle married Gertrude Stoner, raised a family, and lived the rest of his life in Missouri. But as we learn from his daughter, Mary E. Turek, of Grantsburg, Wisconsin, "He was always ashamed of his background." And because of the anguish of separation from his mother and sister and the trauma of the long train ride he "never told us anything."

THOMAS DUNLOP

(From his daughter, Diana Dunlop Laursen, letters to Evelyn Trickel, November 15, 1984; May 15, 1985; and October 25, 1986.)

For Diana Dunlop Laursen, growing up with an Irish father such as Thomas Dunlop was a joyous experience. She was fascinated by his stories of his early life. But he was the Irish storyteller, and which was fact and which was embellished she was never quite sure. Either way, she enjoyed it.

What is fact is that her father came on an orphan train to Keytesville, Chariton County, Missouri, in 1887. This is established by a document still in the family, a letter of introduction signed by Mrs. H. M. Harris, the corresponding secretary of the American Female Guardian Society of New York.

To the parties who may become the guardians of Thomas Dunlop: Dear Friends—The bearer, Thomas Dunlop is sent to you in care of Mr. E. Trott from the above named institution to which [Thomas] has been legally committed. You will find in the enclosed bylaws such items as marked as require special attention. If you desire to keep him or desire to return or relocate him, please let us hear from you as indicated in the bylaws.

The American Female Guardian Society is identified in the letter as an orphan home cooperating with the Children's Aid Society. This accounts for the fact that it was an agent of the Children's Aid Society who accompanied the boy.

As his daughter remembers, "[my father] was supposed to go to General Sterling Price, but my grandmother, Lula Maupin of Prairie Hill begged [for] him for Daddy." Her memory is corroborated by her grandmother: "Sterling Price had sent for boys to help him on his farm. Thomas was to be one of them. But when I saw the darling, black-eyed Irish boy, I begged Mr. Price for him, and somewhat reluctantly, he let Thomas go with us." Agent Trott agreed to this change. (The famous Confederate general, Sterling Price, had died in 1867, twenty years before Thomas Dunlop arrived on the orphan train. Whether this Sterling Price is related to the earlier one is unclear.)

Some five months later, Thomas' foster parents, Lula and A. D. Maupin, received a letter from Mrs. Harris: "We are glad and thankful that Thomas has fallen into a good home," she wrote. In another letter, dated November 1887, Mrs. Harris responded to the family's inquiries about the boy's natural parents. "Tommy was born in the north of Ireland, February 27, 1883. Scotch-Irish Presbyterian the family all were and the mother well connected. The uncle of the mother is a noted Scotch clergyman.

About a year later, Mrs. Harris wrote, "Dear Friends; We hope you have a good report to send us and that Tommy is a comfort and a good little boy." The family looks on these letters through the years as evidence of Mrs. Harris' genuine concern for the boy's welfare.

Though he was never legally adopted, and retained his own surname, Thomas loved his foster parents. But as he grew up he was naturally curious about his own parentage. He always said, his daughter tells us, "The present is no more important than the past." In his efforts to learn of his family he heard a number of stories. One rumor had it that he

Willie Paul Dunnaway with foster parents, Charles and Maggie Dunnaway, near Bentonville, Arkansas, 1916. *(Courtesy W. P. Dunnaway.)*

had been placed in the orphan home in New York City by a young nurse who said that the child's parents had died on shipboard on the way from Ireland to New York. In 1932 a Robert W. Dunlop replied to Thomas' inquiry. "I think I knew your father or his brother. These two brothers came to New York from Belfast. I met Robert Dunlop in 1886. He had a bakery on Bleeker Street, New York. He and his wife disappeared very suddenly in 1887 and no one located them. One of these brothers was probably your father."

The full story of his background was never known. But,

his daughter says, Thomas was always the devoted son to his foster parents. He never lost his sense of humor or his Irish zest for life. Diana Laursen looks on the orphan trains as bringing good fortune to those who rode them.

WILLIE PAUL DUNNAWAY

(From letters to Michael Patrick, August 24, 1985, and September 17, 1985.)

I too rode the train to Bentonville, Arkansas, in 1916, on October 16, 1916. I became the luckiest boy on earth. I was adopted by Charles W. Dunnaway and his wife, Maggie Dunnaway. They had been married several years and had no children, so thanks to the Children's Aid Society I was chosen to become their son.

God in all of his greatness never made any better people than they. They have since gone to their reward.

I married a school classmate in the year of 1931. We raised five children, three boys and two girls. They have all married and live in Benton County, Arkansas. All live within twenty miles of us. They brought us ten grand children and five greats.

In November [1985] we will have been together fifty-four years.

This letter from Willie Dunnaway was accompanied by a photograph and two documents, mementos of that eventful period in his early life. One of the documents is the placing-out certificate from the Children's Aid Society, with a note by Willie: "The man in charge was E. P. Morgan, Wheeler, Ark."

The other is a health certificate, using Willie's original name, Billy Czik. Just before he was placed on the train, the boy was given a physical examination by a Dr. Charles Lapman, who signed the certificate. "This certifies that I have this day examined Billy Czik and find him in good health and free from any contagious and infectious disease."

The photograph is that of Willie's foster parents, smiling contentedly under a tree in the front yard of their farmhouse. The picture was taken in 1916, shortly after the boy's arrival. On it Willie has written, "These are the folks that made me the most fortunate person on earth today."

ANNE FLICKINGER

(Interviewed by Martha Mondell, assistant to Evelyn Sheets, June 5, 1986.)

When Anne Flickinger was only fourteen days old, her mother left her in the New York Foundling Hospital. At four, she fell on a concrete surface and injured her leg, an injury for which she had four operations in the next three years. Because she was bedfast much of the time, she had little opportunity for education. But the nuns treated her very well. Her most vivid memories of that period are the good times she had on outings with the nuns and other children to Coney Island and Central Park. She lived in the Foundling Hospital until she was nine years old.

Then one day, without any notice, the nuns "put an old black and white dress on me and some other children and pinned name cards to the back of our dresses." With the nurses and nuns and "a man" in charge, they were put on a mercy train at Grand Central Station. There were about sixty-five children, Mrs. Flickinger recalls, packed together "like cattle." Her only memory of the trip was that it took "a long time," which no doubt it did, since the destination was Louisiana. There arrangements had been made for the placement of all the children. "I was very unhappy," Anne says, "when I saw I was going with old people in their seventies." The couple took her because their own children were grown and had moved away.

Although she missed the foundling home, she was well treated in Louisiana. Soon after her placement, the new parents took her to a doctor to have something done about her injured leg. It soon began to heal and Anne was able at last to go to school. She attended a country school near the farm where her foster parents raised cotton, cane, corn and cattle. The farm was so self-sufficient that she does not recall having to buy anything at the store.

Because the mother was French, French was the language of the household, and Anne had to learn it quickly. She says with pride that she learned it "right away." Her father, who was Spanish, died three years after she went to live with them. But Anne remembers that he always treated her kindly and brought her a glass of wine every morning before she got up.

From her mother Anne learned French cooking. She remembers well the large family Christmas dinners with turkey, roast pigs, vegetables, and "six or eight layer cakes." She was taught to perform all the tasks of farm life—how to smoke bacon, ham, and sausage and pack them in jars with lard, and how to preserve food in tin cans instead of glass jars.

At the age of fifteen she decided to "get out on her own." Leaving the farm, she went to work nights as a telephone operator. Later she worked in a drug store. Although she was never legally adopted by her foster family, she used their name until she was twenty-one, when she married and started a family of her own.

MATILDA FRANK

(Rose Ellen Rogers)

(From her daughter, Rose Mary Keys, interviewed by Evelyn Sheets, June 4, 1985.)

One day in 1894 a child about two years old was sent west from the New York Foundling Hospital with a cloth identification tag sewn to her petticoat. The tag bore her name, Matilda Frank; her birthdate, December 2, 1892; and her assignment to a Joseph Giller of St. George, Kansas.

One of the stops on the way was Higginsville, Missouri, in Lafayette County. On the day the train pulled in, Charles and Ellen Rogers were just passing the station and they stopped to watch the children getting off. The couple had recently lost their own baby. The minute they saw little Matilda they knew she was meant for them. Though the child was supposed to go on to Kansas, they pleaded with the agent to let her go with them. The agent relented, and Matilda had a new home. She was also given a new name. Though never legally adopted, she became Rose Ellen Rogers.

In 1915, Rose Ellen neé Matilda was engaged to a childhood sweetheart, David Zimmerman, who had arrived in Higginsville on the same train as she. But the engagement ended when Rose Ellen took a job in Kansas City. There she met Lee Cooley, whom she married. They had one daughter, Rose Mary, who is now Rose Mary Keys.

When some time later the couple were divorced, Rose Ellen moved back to Higginsville and the longtime friendship with David Zimmerman was renewed. Once again they were engaged. But this time David moved away, and that was the end of the relationship. Rose Ellen never married again, nor did David.

After her return to Higginsville, Rose Ellen joined her foster parents in their portrait studio, learning photofinishing and other techniques. She continued working in various photography studios until her retirement in 1954.

OTTO DEIM FUHRMAN

(From Jean Brown-Nepsund, great-niece of Chris Fuhrman, letter to Evelyn Sheets, October 5, 1985.)

One day in 1892 Chris Fuhrman went on business to Forest City, Missouri, in Holt County. By chance that was the day an orphan train arrived carrying children of all ages. Chris had gone to Forest City with no thought at all of taking an orphan child home with him. But among them was a very small boy, and Chris kept going back all day to see if anyone had taken him.

At the end of the day, when he was ready to go home, Chris went back one more time. All the older children had been taken, those who could do farm work. But no one wanted the little three-year-old—except Chris, who bought a shawl to wrap him in and drove home. Unbeknownst to his wife, Anna, he left the child wrapped in a bundle on the kitchen table and went out to do the chores. It was, as might be expected, quite a surprise to Anna, and happily a pleasant one. So, without planning for it, the Fuhrmans had acquired a son.

His name was Otto. He was born in New York on Jan-unary 3, 1889, into a German immigrant family by the name of Deim. Shortly after his birth, when his mother died, his father put the large family up for adoption, hoping they would receive care and opportunities which he as a poor immigrant could not give them. They were taken in by the Children's Aid Society, and Otto remained a ward until he was sent west in 1892.

Chris and Anna Fuhrman legally adopted Otto and always treated him as their own son. He attended high school in Oregon, Missouri, and in 1907 was a member of the Oregon High School state championship football team. Following his graduation he went to business college in Chillicothe, and in 1924 was married to Buella Huiatt. They had one daughter, Marylouise. After a temporary move to Wyoming, Otto and Buella returned to Missouri, where they operated a cafe in Oregon until Otto's death in 1941.

CECILIA SHEESHAM BELL GRAHAM

(Interviewed by Evelyn Sheets, October 31, 1985.)

On the same train with Matilda Frank and David Zimmerman were a little girl and her six-year-old brother. The girl, Cecilia, was about three. Her father had died a few months earlier. Her mother, pregnant, and fearing that something might happen to her, left strict instructions that her children be raised as Catholics. A few months later, she too died. Cecilia and her brother were placed in an orphan home and soon thereafter were sent west on a mercy train. Somewhere along the way the two children were separated and never saw each other again.

In Higginsville, Missouri, Cecilia was taken into the home of Frank and Christen Bell, who raised her as their own. Interviewed at the age of ninety-four Cecilia remembered little about the train ride from New York. But the painful memory of separation from her brother was still with her.

SYDNEY HARVEY HARLEY

(From a letter of December 12, 1986, and an interview with Michael Patrick, December 12, 1989.)

My father, who was a longshoreman wanted to keep us, but simply couldn't provide a normal home. Circumstances forced him to put us in the Children's Aid Society Home, because our mother abandoned the family shortly after we moved to New York City from England. He intended to come back for us, but when he finally did come to get us, Emily and I were on a trip headed for Missouri.

The train which brought young Sydney Harvey and his sister Emily to Missouri stopped in Centralia, Boone County, on June 9, 1910. There they were taken by a dentist, Dr. S. E. Harley and his wife Mary.

> I was very lucky. [The Harleys] had tried unsuccessfully for several years to have children. They had decided to adopt. When our train pulled into the station at Centralia, the Harleys were there waiting. . .As they lined us up on the platform at the train station, we were all wondering about what would happen next. Naturally, we all wanted to be adopted.

When Harvey got off the train he was carrying all his belongings in a box from the fashionable New York store, Saks Fifth Avenue. How he came by this particular box he doesn't recall. Nor does he remember why, out of some forty orphans on the platform, the Harleys chose him and his sister. With the hindsight of a good many years, he says drolly, "I was such a handsome devil. That's why they wanted me."

Soon after, Emily went to live with Mrs. Harley's sister and her husband, who adopted the child. Living near each other, the two children were often together and had a happy childhood. "We spent summers at grandfather Burgess's house in Paris, (Mo.) I remember riding the train and the conductor shouting the town names." They also went to grandfather's house for Christmas, Harvey's favorite time of year. He recalls delivering presents on Christmas Day through knee-deep snow. Of Christmas activities at school or church he says, "There were always so many people around, I always got an aisle seat so I could run to the tree and get my gifts."

An enterprising boy, Harvey started a laundry business while he was still in grade school. "I collected all the collars and cuffs, all the hotel and barbershop laundry and sent it in great big boxes to the laundry in Higginsville." His hard work did not prevent him from being a good student. He still has a letter sent to his foster mother from the Children's Aid Society. "I'm glad to hear," the representative wrote, "that one of our boys is at the head of his class." After graduation from high school in 1923 Harvey entered Central Methodist College in Fayette, Missouri. He later attended the University of Missouri and the Chillicothe Business College.

As a child Harvey often spoke to his foster parents of crossing the ocean. They always assumed that he meant crossing the Missouri River on the train, that to a young boy the river must have seemed like an ocean. But as they learned, the children had in reality crossed the Atlantic with their natural parents. Their father had kept in touch with them through the Children's Aid Society. Then one day in 1942, while Harvey was living in Kansas City, his father "just knocked at the door. It was the only time I saw him. He seemed very happy. I just thought it was nice when I saw him. I appreciated the fact when he told us he really didn't intend to leave us."

A few years ago Harvey looked back at the events of his life with some satisfaction and a great deal of gratitude:

My life has been pretty colorful. I have been a cab driver, newspaperman, salesman, photograph[er], and entrepreneur, owning my own company. I have been widowed twice, after being married to two ladies I loved a great deal, and have gotten to travel some.

It's been 76 long years since that little boy stood on the train station platform, waiting for life to happen to him. Even though now I am lonely sometimes, I look back, and am always grateful for those two people who were willing to open their hearts to my sister and me, giving us a home, and the love we so needed.

At this writing Sydney Harvey Harley lives in retirement in Barry County, Missouri, near Table Rock Lake. In his letter of 1986 he wrote, "I am now 81 in very good health and working on reaching 100."

His sister Emily died several years ago.

GUS AND JOHN JAHNE

(From Gus Jahne, interviewed by Evelyn Sheets, May 1, 1985.)

In 1907 Gus Jahne, who was four or five years old, was the youngest boy on an orphan train carrying a carload of children to Missouri. As he recalled, there were thirty boys in one car, including his brother John, who was eight or nine, and four brothers named Lawyer, with whom the Jahne boys were to be friends throughout their lives. Another car held about thirty girls. Most of these children found homes in or

Group from an orphan train, 1908, Andrew County, Missouri. Seated, Gus Jahne; John Jahne to his left; two Lawyer brothers in background.

around Savannah, Missouri. Gus and John were lucky—they were taken together by Mr. and Mrs. Fred Karrasch, farm people who had no children of their own.

The boys grew up on the farm, learning the value of hard work. Gus Jahne was married on June 17, 1928, to Sylvia Mowrey at the Savannah Baptist Church. Their son Gary was born on February 15, 1934. Throughout his working life Gus held a variety of jobs. He was first a cable splicer for the telephone company, then in construction in St. Joseph. During World War II he served in the army as a light tractor operator. His last job before he retired was that of a butcher for Swift and Company in St. Joseph. Gus died in 1985, only a few weeks before the orphan train riders' reunion in Trenton, which he had planned to attend.

His brother John became an educator. He was married to Ora Crawford on July 25, 1922, and taught in a number of rural schools. In 1928 he received a B.S. degree from the

University of Missouri and in 1946, a master's degree from Drake University. During his teaching career he served as superintendent of schools in several Missouri towns—New Point, Pickering, Ravenwood and Quitman. From 1934 to 1937 he was educational adviser to the Civilian Conservation Corps in the Kingman and Mt. Vernon camps.

EDWARD P. KEARNEY

(From an unpublished autobiography loaned by his daughter, Mary K. McClintock.)

On a "bleak November day" in 1905 a mercy train arrived at Fairfield, Vermont, carrying twenty-four orphans. Among them was a boy named Edward Kearney, who was placed with the Thomas Fitzgerald family. In later years he learned why his foster mother had chosen him out of the twenty-four. Her maiden name was Carney, but the family name, while pronounced the same, was originally spelled Kearney. Her father, Daniel Kearney, had come from Ireland with his wife and four children, settled in St. Albans, Vermont, and found work on a section gang for the Central Vermont Railroad. When he collected his first pay envelope, the name on the outside was "Dan Carney," and Carney it remained from then on. As evidence of the change of spelling, Mrs. Fitzgerald displayed a red trunk with the initials "D. K." printed on it in black.

Before the arrival of the mercy train, Mrs. Fitzgerald had looked at the list of orphans' names passed out at St. Patrick's Church. Because Carney and Kearney sound the same, she chose Edward Kearney from the list.

The arrival of the train and his placement with the Fitzgeralds are described in Edward's words:

Each childs name was printed on a strip of cloth, in indelible ink and then stitched onto it's clothing. My name was among them. The prospective parents were on hand with identification papers to take the children with them.

I was met by a kindly faced lady who offered me a cookie. This however, was not just the proper procedure in this public gathering for a loud clamor arose from all sides and meant that cookies had to be passed around to the whole group. Because of train sickness the children were given very little to eat by the nurse in charge and so [we] were very hungry. We left New York City the day before.

As I look back upon this first venture into the world of strangeness I cannot refrain from comparing this shipment of children to Vermont like shipment of livestock. Dairy cattle have tags in their ears for identification and are dispersed to various places.

My new parents adopted a girl of one and one-half years of age who was to be my sister. She was in this same shipment so this made it less lonesome for the both of us. We were bundled into a buggy and rode five miles to Fairfield Center where I was to live. A pile of Blocks [sic] were on the floor and soon my sister and I were busy with them. She being a little delicate and rather sickly after such a trip from New York at that age, she was soon put to bed and I was left alone to explore my new home.

The back kitchen of this large farm house was a source of revelation to me. Besides a churn, a cream separator, and a lot of small hand tools scattered about, there were long traces of yellow corn hanging against the white-washed walls and a number of pumpkins and squash on the floor. Somehow, it was a long time before I believed that a squash was not just a green pumpkin.

Some of the children did not fare as well as Edward and his small foster sister. "While their attendants had done what they could for these young travelers they did not present an altogether pleasant sight for the prospective parents." Some were suffering from motion sickness and others looked unhealthy. Even though pre-arranged placement was the policy of the New York Foundling Hospital, some of the children were rejected by families who had agreed to take them. "I learned later," Edward wrote, "that at least two families backed down from taking their quotas because they didn't like the looks of them or changed their minds for some other reason." One woman reportedly said, "Con-dum-it, I don't know what I was thinking of. I've already raised three boys and a girl and that's enough." One unwanted boy was taken to the parish priest's house and a week later placed with a family of spinsters and bachelors on a trial basis. They did eventually take him permanently. Another couple had planned to take only one child, a boy, but when one of the girls on the train was rejected, the couple took her too.

In accordance with the Catholic policy, each child was accompanied by a document setting forth the legal terms of his indenture. There is a curious gap between Edward's placement in 1905 and the Fitzgerald's signature on the document six years later, on March 2, 1911. It would seem that he was with the foster parents on a rather long trial basis, or that there is an error in the date.

Whatever the reason for the discrepancy, Edward stayed with the Fitzgeralds as a permanent member of the family. He admits to being a lively child, "too frisky in my funmaking." Often, he said, "my ears would ring after being soundly boxed by a firm hand." He believed this boxing to be the reason he was totally deaf in one ear.

When Edward was nine years old, Thomas Fitzgerald died. "I missed him a great deal for a long time, for we would go to-gether to neighboring towns to trade. Had he lived, I would no doubt have finished my education as he seemed to regret his own lack of it."

As it was, Edward's schooling was interrupted a number of times. After finishing the eighth grade he stayed at home for a year before entering high school at St. Michael's in Winooski. It was while attending St. Michael's that he found outlets for his musical talent. He played second violin in the school orchestra, first coronet in the band, and studied piano. He had been playing the piano since he was nine.

Then during the summer before his sophomore year, lightning struck the Fitzgerald dairy barn and burned it to the ground. After that Edward had to stay home again to help his mother. "Mother always felt high school was not essential for success," he writes. But he tried again, even though "it was against her wishes that I started out each morning on a bicycle for St. Albans to attend the old high school. . ." This lasted only until Thanksgiving, when he had to give up again because of the farm work. ". . .at times I looked after [the farm] for practically no wages, it being duly impressed on my mind at various times, all I owed to my parents for their sacrifices in taking me in and so on."

Tired of farm work and finding that picking up jobs about town was "monotonous," he took a job in St. Albans with American Express. The company soon promoted him to their office in Bellows Falls. But winters there were extremely cold, and in December 1918 he decided he would move to Florida. His mother chose to go with him, leaving his foster sister in school in St. Albans. Florida proved a disappointment. The only express business in the area was the Southern Express Company, and Edward could not work for them under his American Express orders.

His music saved the situation. He played the piano in a movie theater and joined the town band. Through contacts there he found various other jobs, and he and his mother stayed through the winter. But in April they returned to Vermont. Edward continued to work at home on the farm and about town until the age of twenty-one, when he became the postmaster in Fairfield.

> One thing which seemed a little strange to me at twenty-one was the fact that within a month after becoming of age, and taking my own name of Kearney, never having been legally adopted, nearly everyone called me by my rightful name. My old school chums from St. Michaels sometimes call me Fitzgerald but somehow the name Eddie Kearney seemed easy for folks to learn and remember.

After three years he resigned the postmastership, finding that a "fourth class office was not remunerative enough for a young man of that age, especially having to pay his board and washing from a small fee." He was married a few years later and moved back home with his wife to look after his foster mother, who was seriously ill. Mrs. Fitzgerald died that year in September.

During the next few years the Kearneys had three children, two daughters, Nancy and Mary, and a son, Gillin. Their father was kept busy as an interior house painter and paper hanger. But the urge for education was still with him, and he enrolled at Bellows Free Academy and finished high school. After graduation he read for the law with a local barrister. Though he never passed the bar examination, he served as an unofficial clerk for several local lawyers. At one time he was elected Tax Collector for East Fairfield and later was supervisor of relief funds given to the poor.

Throughout, he kept on with his music, which was almost a profession. Besides playing the organ for several churches, he provided the music for funerals and weddings and organized minstrel shows.

The mystery of his parentage troubled Edward Kearney most of his life. Though he made several trips to New York, seeking information about them, he was never successful. Nevertheless, he could write:

> . . .I have given much thought to whether or not children are handicapped by not having known parents living. I have come to the conclusion that I can become what I wish, and not follow a profession such as Doctor or something I dislike because father or uncle was such a man. Neither can anyone point out any member of my family tree with the finger of scorn because they were wayward. After all, where is the family whom some crank cannot point out as having a relative that was [not] quite up to par?

Edward Kearney died in 1979, leaving the rest of his memoirs and his down-home philosophy unrecorded.

THE LAWYER BROTHERS

(Alclo, James, Noah and Stoddard Arthur)

(From Noah and Stoddard Arthur Lawyer, interviewed by Michael Patrick, September 1, 1985, and an unpublished memoir by Alclo's wife, Gladys Lawyer.)

The four Lawyer brothers, sons of a blind farmer, grew up to lead varied lives. One of them owned a flourishing nightclub; one went from farming into the construction business; another became a candidate for Mr. America; and the fourth went off with a circus.

Around the turn of the century these four, with a younger brother named Perry Paul, lived with their parents on a farm near Middleburg, New York. While the youngest one was only a baby, their mother left their father, taking the baby with her. The family never saw her again.

Left with the older boys, their father, Harvey Andrew Lawyer, tried to take care of them and send them to school. But only one boy at a time could go to school in the winter, because there was only one coat and one pair of boots among them. Eventually the grandparents took the boys to live with them. Then in 1907 the grandfather died. The grandmother was ill, and because of this and their father's blindness, the state placed the four boys in an orphanage.

Shortly after that, the Children's Aid Society, having custody of the boys, put them on an orphan train bound for Missouri. It was a long, hard trip. As Alclo recalled, the seats were hard and stiff-backed, covered with something velvety-looking which actually was a "very stickery substance, like lying on pins." The train ran day and night, except for occasional stops where the children were allowed to get off and run and play. At some of these stops people came to look them over and perhaps take one of the orphans. At last the Lawyer brothers with several other children, including Gus and John Jahne, arrived in Sedalia, Missouri. From there J. W. Swan took the group to Savannah, in Andrew County.

Of all the hurtful experiences which could befall the children of the orphan trains, two of the worst were rejection and separation. The young Lawyers experienced both. When the children got off the train in Savannah, all of them were chosen by new parents—all but four, the four little brothers, who were left standing alone. No one had chosen them. When at last Mr. Swan had found someone to take them, they were not taken together but sent to four different homes. Not till they were grown would they come together again as a family.

At first, neither Alclo nor his brother James found a permanent home, but were moved from place to place. Taken by farming families, they were kept out of school as soon as the ground could be plowed in spring. Alclo had a particularly hard time of it. In one home he was not only overworked but poorly fed. At mealtime he was allowed one serving of food and that was it. The natural son could help himself to all he wanted, while the orphan, no matter how hungry, could only sit and watch.

Fortunately, an agent for the Children's Aid Society had wind of this mistreatment. Dressed informally, as if he were just another farmer, the agent dropped in to see the foster family. The father, taking the agent to be a casual visitor from the neighborhood, complained that the boy they had taken was "not much." Alclo was promptly taken away from him and moved to a new family.

By the time of World War II, Alclo was old enough to join the army. After the war he farmed on his own in Andrew

County, where he married Gladys Sabin, the daughter of a family with whom he had lived and worked for a time. Subsequently the couple moved to St. Joseph. Both Alclo and his brother Stoddard Arthur had jobs there and Alclo then went into the construction business.

James Lawyer, called Jim, also went into the service during the war. He was married later, moved to Michigan, and opened a nightclub. He remained in Michigan until his death in the 1970s.

Alclo's wife, Gladys, feels that of the four brothers, Noah Alwoeth was the most fortunate. He was placed only once, taken by a dairy farmer whose first name was Robert. The boy was also called Robert and treated as a son. However, Noah's own version of his childhood is somewhat different. His foster father had seven other orphan boys helping milk his cows. He often made promises he did not keep, and Noah often ran away—only to be lured back by more promises. At school he was teased and abused because he was an orphan. He finally left for good and went off to become a wrestler in a circus.

But after he was married, Noah went back to work again for his foster father. Gladys Lawyer remembers those days:

> We rode the milk wagon with Noah. All through the years we were very close, Noah and Alclo and families. We had weekend ice cream parties at the dairyman's home. That place was always full of the boys who were sent to Andrew County [by the Children's Aid Society]. We almost forgot the slow, uncomfortable train ride. The four scared little boys had managed to keep friends with the others who had been on the train.

Gus Jahne was one of those with whom the Lawyer brothers kept in touch. As Gladys recalls, Gus "was often with Noah Alwoeth Lawyer and his wife, visiting at my parents' home, where the man I married, Alclo Andrew Lawyer, was working and living."

After a brief period on the dairy farm, Noah and his wife moved to New York, but came back every year to visit.

The fourth brother, Stoddard Arthur, was placed with the family of a mail carrier, who also farmed. Though he was obliged to work hard, Stoddard was treated well. In high school he became an outstanding athlete. Had it not been for a leg injury, he believes he might have made the Olympic track team. In Gladys Lawyer's account, ". . .he later took physical education at the YM[CA] and was well into body-building, and became a candidate for 'Mr. America.'"

Stoddard left home as soon as he could and was out of touch with his brothers for sixteen years. It was not until the spring of 1965 that the four of them got together again for a reunion.

During his years away, Stoddard was married. After his wife's death some years later he went to live with his son and daughter-in-law in Arkansas.

Alclo died March 5, 1977.

His surviving brothers, Stoddard and Noah, agreed that, circumstances being as they were, they probably would not have survived if they had remained in New York. They remembered the miseries of that time when the only clothes they had were nothing but sacks. Despite hardships that followed, they are thankful for the orphan train which took them west and allowed them a chance to live.

CLARETTA CARMAN MILLER

(From Mrs. Miller's unpublished autobiography, written because "We are a part of history.")

She began life on March 3, 1908, as Claretta Helen Brown. That was in Elmira, New York, where her father William worked for a coal company for the Pennsylvania Railroad and "drank up most of his pay."

> The old house I was born in was in bad shape. It leaked like a sieve, and we had very little in the way of furniture. We had only one bed and some old dirty mattresses on the floor. The house was overrun with rats, and many a night we woke up screaming because they ran over our beds and many times through our hair. This may sound far-fetched, but I assure you it is true.

When their mother also took to drink, Claretta and her two sisters were sometimes left with an old untrustworthy bachelor uncle. They suffered from the cold and malnutrition and were often sick. They had head and body lice. By the time the welfare department found them, Claretta and her older sister Jeanette had double mastoid ("I was the worst case and nearly bled to death before surgery could be performed"), and Jeanette had developed tuberculosis.

Claretta has no idea how the welfare people knew about them. But the three girls were taken from their parents at once. "Some very kind people took us, cleaned us up, burned our old clothing, and we were taken to an Italian cafe. I recall my first taste of spaghetti. It has been one of my favorite dishes through the years. I also recall having a pretty ribbon for my hair."

After being "nursed back to a degree of health" at the Southern Tiers Children's Home in Elmira, Jeanette was sent to a sanitarium in White Plains, New York, where she eventually recovered. Claretta and her younger sister Geraldine were sent to live on a farm with a couple named Grover. They had been there less than a year when Geraldine was taken into the home of Mrs. Grover's niece, who later adopted the child. "About this time," Mrs. Miller writes, "Mrs. Grover discovered she was about to produce her own family and was therefore no longer able to keep me." Claretta was picked up again by a welfare lady and this time taken to New York City to an all-girls' home run by the Children's Aid Society.

> At that time World War I was raging in Europe, and I can vaguely recall seeing big blimps drifting slowly overhead when we were allowed out in the courtyard to play games.
> We had a very strict superintendent, but she also had a soft heart and was very good to all of us. I was there about nine months or so. We were always clean and well fed—never mistreated. There was a classroom where we held school. One evening at the supper table we were told to gather in the classroom. There we were informed that we were going on a journey the next day. We were to take our baths that night, and were issued all new clothes. We had no idea where we were going, only that it was a long way and we would travel by train.

Only when they were aboard—some two hundred children —did they learn that they were on "The Orphan Train." They traveled for three days and two nights, bound for Omaha, Nebraska. The girls rode in one coach, accompanied by two unmarried sisters, later identified as Mary and Alice Bogardus of Sedalia, Missouri. The brother of these two traveled in another coach with the boys. One of the orphans in the girls' coach was a baby, eight or nine months old.

We changed trains in Chicago and arrived in Omaha on a very cold, windy morning. We were taken to the Old Opera House where we were fed, and then put on the stage to sit in a semi-circle. The people were notified in advance of our arrival and were waiting for us. We were allowed to talk to some of them, and they told us about their homes, etc.

I was sent home with a German family, who neglected to say anything about their own family. Come to find out, they already had nine, with one midget who was mean. I was made to wait on them. I was there only two weeks when I was taken away and sent to Ashland, Nebraska, about thirty or forty miles from Omaha. I remained there during the summer, but can't recall the names of the people I stayed with.

Because Claretta was not a very healthy child, people were reluctant to keep her very long. In the early fall she was removed from the second home to that of a widow who took in orphans on a temporary basis until permanent homes could be found for them. While there, Claretta came down with a bad case of "World War I flu," had a relapse, and remained with the widow until after Christmas.

It was then that a significant change occurred. An older couple, Mr. and Mrs. Marcus Carman, who lived near Cook, Nebraska, had been looking for a boy to live with them. But all the boys from that orphan train had been taken. Claretta was the last child left without a permanent home. The ladies in charge of the orphans' placement then went to see the couple. The Carmans lived on an eighty-acre farm, but both of them, well-educated, had taught school for twenty-five years, and Mr. Carman had been a County Superintendent of Schools. When they heard about the little girl who needed a home, they agreed to take her on trial.

This was the beginning for me, and a blessing. I was a lost and lonely child, just eight years old, not very well, and a long way from home, among total strangers. I arrived at the Carman farm after dark on a rainy night by horse and buggy. When I was put to bed that night the flood gates opened wide and I cried my heart out. It had been long overdue. Mrs. Carman never had any children of her own and had a heart as big as all outdoors. She stayed with me until the tears were over and I at last fell asleep. The next morning things looked a lot brighter. It took me a year with 'tender loving care' to get going again.

That Christmas, 1919, she saw her first Christmas tree and was given her first doll. Until then, she says, "I didn't know there was a Santa Claus."

In summer "They turned me loose. . .out there. I was too young to work, so I spent the summer playing with the animals." Soon she had lambs and calves tagging after her. There were cats and kittens to play with and "three adorable fox terrier dogs and puppies." She had a horse to ride and was given a Holstein calf to raise, to show at the County Fair. "I worked faithfully to raise that calf but just a month before Fair time the calf got 'black leg' and we couldn't save it. I was heart broken." But she was then given a pig to raise, and the following year her pig and a pen of piglets won second prize. "That ended my career in livestock," she writes.

Meanwhile, she was going to school and studying music. She learned to play the piano, and she and her foster mother sang duets. The Carmans bought an Edison phonograph and Claretta sang opera along with the recordings by Madame Schumann-Heinke and Caruso.

One summer in the early Twenties the Carmans hired a young helper by the name of James Leander Douglass. When she was eighteen Claretta married the young man. They had two children, a boy and a girl. Until the Depression forced them out, they lived on farms and ranches. James Douglass then went to work for the Union Pacific Railroad, while Claretta worked in cafes. Her husband was a Master Mason and both of them joined the Order of the Eastern Star. In 1972 Claretta became Worthy Matron of Avesta Chapter in Elgin, Nebraska, and she remained active in the organization until 1984. Meanwhile, her husband had retired because of ill health and had died.

Several years later, Claretta was married again. Ray James Miller was a rodeo performer. He stood 6' 2", and with his father, a brother, and two sisters was part of a rodeo act, "The Miller Family," that did trick riding and fancy roping.

He and his brother Alva were the only performers to jump two horses together through frames of fire. Mrs. Miller "lost Ray to cancer, but memories linger on."

Now in her eighty-first year, Mrs. Miller lives in Longmont, Colorado, "among many friends who are wonderful people," enjoying "the view of the mountains and the social events as they come along." Although she lives in a retirement home, she is far from retired. In addition to her hobbies —she sews, makes dolls, pieces quilts and quilts them by hand —she attends Longs Peak Methodist Church and sings with a group known as the Hoverettes.

And she has now begun a new career. This grandmother to nine, great-grandmother to twenty-nine, and great-great-grandmother to eight, has become a public speaker, appearing before school groups and various organizations to talk of her long, eventful life. Two newspapers, the Longmont *Times-Call,* and the Denver *Post,* have carried feature stories about her. And indeed this "orphan from an Orphan Train" has quite a story to tell.

FRANK MITCHELL

(From his son-in-law, R. C. Jack, letter addressed to Evelyn Sheets, September 30, 1986 [handed on to Evelyn Trickel].)

Like most of the children who rode the orphan trains, Frank Mitchell was moved precipitously from an urban to a rural environment—from Boston to an Iowa farm. He was placed with Mr. and Mrs. Michael Mitchell, Irish Catholics, who lived near the town of Dysart. After his foster father died, Frank continued to live on the farm. Even while working in nearby Waterloo, he made his home with his foster mother until his marriage. He then moved with his wife to Des Moines.

It would appear that Frank enjoyed his first train ride. We know, at least, that he made railroading his career. He worked first on the Illinois Central, later on the Rock Island line.

"We knew relatively little about him," Frank's son-in-law, R. C. Jack, wrote. "We are lacking in details because, apparently, he was not close to the family in later years.

There was at least one other son [in the Mitchell family], apparently a natural son and I believe he inherited the family farm." In a postscript to his letter, Mr. Jack wrote that even though Frank was not close to the foster parents, "It may . . .be significant that [he] named his only son Michael."

DANIEL MORGAN

(From his son, Paul D. Morgan, letter to Evelyn Sheets, August 20, 1985.)

In 1943, while Paul D. Morgan was in training at the Coast Guard Sound School in New London, Connecticut, he visited the New York Foundling Hospital to inquire about his father's ancestry. A few weeks later his father, Daniel Morgan, received the following letter:

PLACING OUT DEPARTMENT

Kindly refer to
#6739-B

December 27, 1943

Mr. Daniel Morgan
550 Finkman Street
St. Louis 9, Missouri

Dear Mr. Morgan:
A few weeks ago, your son, Paul, visited this office to inquire for information on your history. We advised him that this information would be forwarded directly to you.

According to our records, you were admitted to this Institution on December 16, 1875, when you were left by your mother, who gave your name as Daniel Morgan, age as two weeks old, and stated that you had been baptized. Your date of birth in our records is carried as December 2, 1875.

Since your mother was unable to provide for you, she requested that you be placed for adoption with the hope that you would receive the care and advantages that she would want for you but could not give you. You were therefore placed by this Institution on June 1, 1880 in the home of Anton Terver, of St. Libori, St. Cloud County, Illinois.

We regret exceedingly that the information on your early history is so meagre. Since no inquiries or visits were made for you, after leaving you here, there has been no opportunity for us to supplement the information above given.

Praying God to bless you and your family with His

125

choicest graces, and extending to you and yours our best wishes for a Happy and Prosperous New Year, I am

Very truly yours,
Sister Agnita Miriam, Supt.
NEW YORK FOUNDLING HOSPITAL

vb

From Paul Morgan we learn more about his father's life: In Daniel's foster home, as in the school he attended, German was the only language spoken. By the age of ten he had learned to speak and read German very well.

> In later years some may have thought this incongruous, given his name with strong Welsh ties. Dad always thought of himself as being of Welsh descent, mainly because of his name; he had no knowledge of his forebears. He often spoke of the meaning of his name, 'dweller by the sea.'

Living in southern Illinois, Daniel was far from the sea. But while the "regimen on the farm was strict, Dad indicated that it was a reasonably happy time."

At the age of eighteen or nineteen Daniel left the farm, settled in St. Louis, and was married. Shortly after the birth of their daughter, his wife died. Leaving the child with his foster sister, Anna Luechtefeld, he set out for the far west. He traveled through Nevada and California and other parts of the West as a collector for a magazine and returned to St. Louis with a lifelong interest in and knowledge of geography.

In 1916 he married Josephine Bradac. The couple had three children. Robert, the eldest, born in 1917, became a scientist and worked in the Manhattan project directly under J. Robert Oppenheimer. Paul, the second son, was born in 1919, followed two years later by a daughter, Charlotte.

"Though we were far from wealthy," Paul wrote, "we survived the Great Depression of the 1930's; I pay tribute to my Dad for always having an income from his newspaper route through those tough times." Since Daniel always kept in touch with his foster relatives, the family visited them fairly often.

Daniel Morgan, who rode an orphan train at the age of five, lived to be eighty-five. He died in 1960. Robert, his oldest son, died in 1977, daughter Helen, by his first wife, two years later. Charlotte, who had four children, presently lives in Kansas City.

EDWARD NEWMAN

(Interviewed by Evelyn Sheets, November 12, 1984.)

Rejection became a familiar story to a small boy who arrived in Trenton, Grundy County, Missouri, in 1929. Nine-year-old Edward Newman and his brother Peter were passengers on one of the last orphan trains. The children were placed in the home of Dolph Smith, but soon after, the Smiths decided they could not keep both of the boys. They chose Peter, because he was big enough to work, and asked the western placing-out agent to take Edward back to New York.

The agent was the Reverend J. W. Swan, whom the boys called Grandpa Swan. A caring and conscientious man, Swan found another home for Edward in Jamesport, Davies County, with a family named Waddell. For some reason the boy did not stay there long but was moved into the Hatcher family. Edward "truly loved" living with the Hatchers because he had "lots of toys to play with." But as his story goes, he "hung around men who used foul language," and the Children's Aid Society removed him. He was taken back to Trenton, where he stayed in the Old Plaza Theatre building, waiting to be returned to New York as a child who could not be placed.

But Edward was to have one more chance. Before he could be sent back, Mr. Swan had notice from a family in Tindall in Grundy County, that they would try the boy. It was four miles from Trenton to Tindall. The boy traveled there by taxi—only to find when he reached the farm of W. D. Hack that he was unwanted. The Hacks found him too small.

So many rejections and removals were more than any child should have to endure, and Edward had had enough. Faced with the alternative of an orphanage in New York, he "sold himself" to the Hacks. He was small, but he promised them he would grow. And grow he did. The Hacks took his word, took the boy in, and he lived with them until 1941, when he married and made a home of his own.

ROBERT PETERSEN

(From an interview with Michael Patrick, April 16, 1990.)

. . .probably the luckiest day of my life was when I was abandoned in that train station in Philadelphia. . .

Such a provocative opening promises a good story, and in spite of some bleak moments, it is a happy story that Robert Petersen goes on to tell. His abandonment, he says, was "the first step on my road to a wonderful new life with a wonderful new family."

Of his natural parents he has no real memory. All he knows is what someone told him later on. When his mother died, the children were left with their father, whose situation was "very erratic." He was sometimes rich and sometimes poor. "I don't know what happened when he walked away from us in that train station. . .but I assume it was probably one of his lower moments."

My first really vivid memory is sitting on a stage in the meeting hall in Blair, Nebraska, waiting for someone to choose me, but no one did. It was a terrible Saturday night. It was 1923, and I was six years old. I know I felt terrible that night because I also remember feeling very happy two days later when the agent took me out to a farm and a family agreed to keep me.

The Children's Aid Society agent was Alice Bogardus, and apparently she had hustled around on Monday morning and found families for the children who weren't chosen on Saturday night. My family, the Petersens, hadn't come on Saturday because they were afraid they were too old, so they were very happy to have a chance to get a child.

The Petersens were farm people, but the boy was not taken as a farm hand. "I was taken as a son. This was made so obvious to me from the very beginning."

After graduating from high school, Robert Petersen attended Creighton University in Omaha, where he now practices law. Of his three children one is a boy adopted when he was "about eleven or twelve. . .I adopted him for two reasons. I didn't have a boy. I had two girls and I wanted a boy. And again, my adoption had been such a lucky event for me, I wanted to do the same for someone else."

THE RIFENBURGH CHILDREN

(Howard Darnell, Lucy, Steven, Virgil and Nelson)

(From Howard's daughter, Joyce Duval, and his widow, Mattie Darnell Stroker, interviewed by Evelyn Sheets, June 4, 1985, and Michael Patrick, July 16, 1989.)

In the spring of 1910 an orphan train pulled in to Bowling Green, Missouri, carrying four children by the name of Rifenburgh. That same day Mr. and Mrs. W. P. Darnell of nearby Curryville had come to town with no knowledge of the train's arrival. They didn't even know what an orphan train was. But out of curiosity they went to the courthouse to watch the children being selected.

"A chunky little boy," not yet four years old, ran up to Mr. Darnell, hugged his leg, and pleaded, "Mister, won't you take me?" The Darnells had no intention of taking an orphan into their home, and they went away without him. But not long after, as he was chatting with the local druggist, Mr. Darnell said he would take "the little fat boy if he was not already spoken for." With this, little Howard Rifenburgh went home with the Darnells, with whom he lived until he was grown. He was the only one of five Rifenburgh children who did not have to change foster homes over the next few years, and the only one to be legally adopted.

This story comes from Howard's daughter, Joyce Duval. Joyce is one of five children born to Howard and his wife Mattie Holman, whom he married in 1925. Howard died in 1945, but his widow, later Mrs. Stroker, now widowed for the second time, has done much to reconstruct and preserve her first husband's family history.

Howard was born in 1906 in Middleburg, New York. A few months after his birth his mother died, leaving the father to care for eight children. After three and a half years, "he was faced with the reality of being unable to provide adequately for the children's needs, even though the older children were able to care for themselves. So in the middle of the Christmas holidays of 1909, he gathered the five younger

129

children together and delivered them into the care of the Children's Aid Society of New York."

There is a touching aside to the story. On that December day, when the Society's representative came for the children, their father put an axe over his shoulder and walked off into the woods. Little Nelson, who was five years old, watched him go, and that is the last he remembers of his father.

The removal of the younger ones also deeply affected their older brother Edwin. The night before they were to be taken away, Edwin ran away from home. He walked thirty miles before he stopped at a farm house. When asked about his age, he lied and said sixteen. Whether the family believed him of not, they let him stay, and he remained with them for the next three years.

Soon after they were taken by the Children's Aid Society, four of the children were sent westward on an orphan train.

Lucy, 14, Steven, 12, Virgil, 9, and Nelson, 5, rode the train to Lebanon, Missouri, in Laclede County, where they were placed in temporary homes. Howard remained in New York at that time because he was hospitalized for treatment of bronchitis.

Within a few months, however, Howard had recovered enough to follow his sister and brothers. In the meantime, the homes where Lucy, Virgil, and Nelson had been placed had proved unsatisfactory, and the train carrying Howard stopped in Lebanon to pick them up.

Steven, who remained in Lebanon, was at the train station that day in March of 1910 to see his siblings off to their new homes. That was the last time Steven ever saw them except for Howard with whom he reunited in 1936.

The four children were deposited in Bowling Green, where "the little fat boy" was taken by the Darnells. Lucy was raised by an older couple by the name of McCormick. When she was eighteen she returned to New York, where she married Howard Wheelock. Virgil, raised by a couple named Burkholder, joined the navy as a young man. Nelson, who had already been moved from one foster home, was placed with Mr. and Mrs. George Howard and moved a second time when that proved unsatisfactory. He then went to live on a farm with Mr. and Mrs. Sam Ray. Although he was never legally adopted, he took the name of his foster parents and became Nelson Ray.

Steven was also moved from his first placement, from Lebanon to Conway, where he lived with Mr. and Mrs. Joel Davis. In recent years his son Lawrence Rifenburgh has been the sheriff of Laclede County for two terms.

Nelson, Lucy, and their older brother Edwin were fortunate to meet each other again in the 1960s, when Nelson made two trips to New York. Later Edwin visited him in Missouri. By that time, both Steven and Howard had died, Howard in 1948, Steven three years earlier.

In her research Mrs. Stroker has found many variations in the spelling of the family name. They include Ryphenberger, Reifenberg, Rightenburgh, Risenbarek, Rifenbough and Rivenberg. Rifenburgh remains the most common spelling, along with Rivenberg. She attributes these variations to the illiteracy of early immigrants. Many of them could neither read nor write, and ship captains and immigration officers simply spelled the names the way they sounded.

Although she has been widowed for the second time and has suffered two strokes, Mattie Darnell Stroker continues her genealogical research into the family of her first husband.

On the whole, in character, the Rifenburghs were simple, hard working, honest, temperate, active, family oriented people. Most of them stress education, decency, Christian living. Some of them have married several times. In personality, the females are stern and talkative, the males are stern and quiet. Both tend to domineer, possibly because they take responsibilities so seriously. Always, work before pleasure! They seem to be mentally, physically, and economically healthy. The characteristics are exactly like all the children of the Rifenburghs I have ever known.

DEBORAH AND KATHLEEN SCOTT

(From Kathleen's daughter, Betty Moore, interviewed by Evelyn Sheets, June 4, 1985.)

On June 26, 1905, the following story appeared in the Gallatin, Missouri, newspaper:

FOUND HOMES

Good homes were found for the ten children brought here from New York by Rev. J. W. Swan last Thursday. There were so many applications for the children that the trouble of the local committee was mostly confined to making selections that would be to the best interests of the children and their foster parents. The meeting was advertised for the Y. M. C. A. rooms and they proved entirely too small and a change was made to the Cumberland Presbyterian Church, the use of which was generously proffered by Rev. H. F. Smith. Every seat in the large church was occupied. It was indeed an affecting scene as the little ones were divided out, though so far as possible those of the same family were sent into the same neighborhood. There were two bright little sisters, and fortunately an application for both of them was made by M. A. Scott, a wealthy farmer living near Lock Springs in Livingston County and the committee was unanimous in placing them with him. Mrs. William Koch, T. H. Wilson, I. J. Vogelsang and J. W. Marshall of Gallatin were given children, Wm. Gutherie of Jameson, a Mr. Carter and two Mr. Godwins in the Jamesport neighborhood were among the fortunate ones. The homes are among the best in the county.

The day the train arrived in Gallatin, Mrs. M. A. Scott had gone to the station prepared to take one girl. When she saw the two "bright little sisters" clinging to each other, she could not bear to see them separated. As she told her family, "I had to take them both."

The Scotts had begun adoption procedures when their lawyer made a discovery. The sisters, Deborah and Kathleen, had come from a wealthy New York family named Reed, and their mother was still living. The story was this:

While their parents were traveling in Europe, Deborah and Kathleen had been left in New York with a governess. The parents sent money for their upkeep, but after a time, when the money stopped coming in, the governess apparently lost touch with the parents. Having no one to contact about the children, she turned them over to the Children's Aid Society. Under New York law they became wards of the state and were placed in an orphanage, from where the Society sent them on to Missouri on an orphan train.

Eventually, the mother, now separated from her husband, came back to New York. Finding her daughters gone, she hired a detective, who located them in Missouri living with their foster parents. Legally the Scotts were obliged to return the children to their mother. In spite of their emotional attachment to the girls, and the girls' tears, they were preparing to send them back. Then their mother decided that Deborah and Kathleen would be better off with the Scotts, and the children stayed. But because of possible legal entanglements and fear that the sisters might lose their inheritance, the Scotts were advised against adopting them.

Throughout their childhood, the girls' mother continued to send them gifts from her travels. Only when she was dying did she ask that her daughters be sent to her. Though Kathleen went to see her mother, Deborah did not.

The sisters grew up and married men from the Gallatin area. Deborah's daughter, Betty Moore, the only surviving member of the family, still has many heirlooms from her mother's experience and that of her aunt on the orphan train. Among them is the card which was pinned to the collar of her mother's dress, giving her name, her age (8), and the date of placement—June 25, 1905.

IRMA CRAIG SCHNIEDERS

(From Mrs. Schnieders' unpublished memoirs, in which she recounts her experiences and mentions twenty other orphan train riders whom she knew.)

I was born in New York according to my birth records from St. Vincent's Foundling Hospital, on the 5th day of July, 1898. My father's name was Walter Craig and my mother's name was Lida Steinberg Craig. My father was a draftsman and was 43 years old at the time of my birth. I was brought to the Foundling Home when I was 58 days old by my mother, and I was baptized on Sept. 6, 1898. I haven't been able to get any records of my parents whereabouts after that.

The orphans were 'indentured,' meaning that a couple signed an agreement, not legal, that they would treat the child well. I was placed with a couple named George and Katherine Boehm on May 19, 1901. Sr. Evlyn [Mrs. Schnieders' daughter] had an interview with Sr. Augustine at the Foundling Hospital located at St. Vincent Ferrer parish, in a very elite district, and she told Sr. Evlyn how a sister would take between 20 and 40 little ones on the train in response to several Pastors' finding good homes for the children. How it was a struggle to get fresh milk for a long trip, especially when spending the night at a railroad siding. Sometimes the sisters would make the social service calls themselves, sometimes it was done by hired local people, and often by the parish priest.

I was about 33 months old, when with 35 others, I arrived at the Osage [Missouri] railroad station. Mrs. Boehm would tell how I had accepted her and had said: 'This is my mama.' I'm sure the sisters had prepared us for this meeting before. Some of the children were barely 18 months old, and some were 4 and 5 years old. Cecelia Titus was almost four, recalls how she resisted going to her new parents, Mr. and Mrs. Henry Sommers from Osage Bend, and had said: 'That's not my mama.' When they stopped at Plasemeyer's Store at Wardsville, Mr. Plasemeyer asked them if that was their new little girl, Cecelia piped up and quickly said, 'But I'm not going to stay with them.' When they were ready to go home they found Cecelia upstairs, she says that she remembers looking for Charley, her playmate at the orphan home. I didn't remember that day very long, but I always did know that I was an orphan. Henry Sommers had also adopted a boy, Joe, but he was several years older, and his son Vincent is living at Wardsville.

The following are names of those that I knew, but some were taken to Jefferson City, and not all kept their own names:

1—Joe Renterghem with the Renterghem family at Osage Bend
2—Helen Renterghem with the Renterghem family at Osage Bend
3—Cecelia Titus with the Hyl Sommer family at Osage Bend
4—Therese Sommer with the John Sommer family at Osage Bend
5—Iona Kane with the John Schmidt family at Osage Bend (later with the Otto Kroeger family. She was high spirited and needed patience. She became a sister.)
6—Walter Adrian with the Herman Adrian family at Osage Bend
7—Carl Adrian with the Herman Adrian family at Osage Bend
8—Joe Markway with the Fred Markway family at Wardsville
9—Alice Gangwich with the Gangwich family at Wardsville

10—Joe Laux with the Laux family at Jefferson City

11—Edna Laux with the Laux family at Jefferson City

12—Oscar Fischer with the Steve Ortmeyer's family at Taos [Missouri] (drowned while in service)

13—Tom Carter with the Ben Prenger family at Taos (When great grandma Prenger saw how he was treated and how unhappy he was, she took him and sent him through school. Then he stayed with Will Wolters until he was on his own. He liked his home there, and came to see me in 1951 when I was working at St. Mary's Hospital. He never forgot the Wolters family. He suffered so much before he died in 1971.)

14—Mary Rhinehart, went to the Steve Ortmeyer family at Taos. She was a sweet girl, took care of Mrs. Ortmeyer during her long illness. She died of tuberculosis.

15—Annie Meyer, was taken by Ben Forck family. She married Herman Taube, and was accidently shot by one of her young boys.

16—Mary Ryan went to the Alphonse Lootens family at Taos. They were an elderly family who had emigrated from Belgium. Mary left the church after she married, had one daughter, and died in the late 1960's.

17—Magdalene Donner was raised by Fr. Joseph Schmidt and his housekeeper, Helena Sutterer. She had beautiful, dark red hair, and was fun to be with. She married Lawrence Weckenborg, whose mother had also been an orphan and was raised by Fr. Schmidt or by the former pastor, Fr. Grounder; who also sent for his young niece, from Germany, Mrs. Eliz. Frank and raised her. Magdalene's son, Lonnie, is a partner of Audivox Hearing Aids in Jefferson City.

18—Frances Brogan was raised by Miss Lizzie Eiken (a great aunt of Ralph Eiken). She married Tony Stegeman, and one of her sons is Archie Stegeman.

19—Marian Beck was first taken by Mr. and Mrs. John Herman of Taos. She later went to John's parents, and was a lovely girl with red hair and one of my best friends. While she was working in Kansas City she took a course in stenography and then married her boss, a lawyer. They came to visit us when we were living in the bottom. She died of cancer.

20—Julia Pebble went to the Frank Watts family at Taos. They were the great grandparents of Gladys Bernskoetter. Julia was a homely child, but could learn well in school. She married Conrad Koetting, a cousin of Art Schults. He was a bachelor, they had several children and the only boy died in World War II, and her mother's family have the Joannes Hatchery on Highway 50 East.

21—My name was Irma Craig, and I went to George and Katie Boehm. She died in May, 1909, and I went to live with the John Rackers family.

In her autobiography Mrs. Schnieders goes on to say that she graduated from the eighth grade in 1913. After going back for a year of review, she took the examination for a teacher's certificate to teach in the county schools. The first year she taught at Schnieders Bridge School for forty dollars a month. The following year she received the magnificent sum of forty-five dollars a month.

In 1922, when she was twenty-four, she married Robert Schnieders. After his death in 1939 she moved with her children to Jefferson City, where she makes her home today. Five of her children live in that area: Don, Edgar, Stanley, Shirley Andrews and Sister Evlyn, of the staff of the office of religious education. Her daughter Mitzi Lindsenhardt lives in Sedalia, another daughter, Helen Cook, in Olathe, Kansas, and her son Robert in Sweet Springs, Missouri.

LOUIS VALLIERES SKIDMORE

(As told by his daughter, Rosalie Skidmore Wilcox, in a letter to Evelyn Sheets, June 24, 1985.)

When an orphan train stopped in Skidmore, Missouri, one day in 1911, all the children were taken to new homes—except one small boy. Louis Vallieres was left on the platform. But among those who had gathered at the meeting place was a young girl who, seeing that the boy was the only one left, ran home and persuaded her mother to come back with her and meet the child. Her mother agreed to take him home that night on a trial basis. And so it was that, through the compassion of young Ella Skidmore, Louis Vallieres joined the family of R. A. and Rebecca Skidmore and soon became a permanent member.

Louis' father had been a chef on a French ocean liner. Rosalie, his mother, had operated a laundry in New York. After the death of her husband she married again but died a short time later. The stepfather then placed Louis and his

Louis Vallieres Skidmore. *(Courtesy Rosalie Skidmore Wilcox.)*

three-year-old sister in one of the Children's Aid Society homes. The little girl, called Rosalie after her mother, was sent to the Midwest alone, ahead of her brother. Although he searched for her all his life, he never found her.

Nor did he ever forget that woeful experience of being the last child chosen. But he always thought of the orphan train as bringing him good fortune. Landing by chance with the Skidmore family gave him an opportunity in life.

The Skidmores never legally adopted me; however, I have always used the name Louis Vallieres Skidmore and there was never any objections to my knowledge. I was proud of their name and wanted them proud of me for using their name.

None of the Skidmores are living at present [1962]. Ella Skidmore Sewell, daughter of Mrs. Rebecca Skidmore, who chose me to stay with her mother died December 26, 1958. Age 88.

Louis attended the University of Missouri, majoring in veterinary medicine. After teaching at Kansas State University, he joined the faculty of the University of Nebraska. He remained there for thirty-eight years and by his estimate taught over twenty-two thousand students.

His daughter, Rosalie, named for his mother and lost sister, remembers her father as "a humanitarian and animal lover."

His three great loves in life were first, his family; second teaching and working with students and young people; third, caring for animals.

When I was growing up, I remember many of the neighborhood children would bring their pets and other animals to 'Doc'—birds with broken wings, baby rabbits they had found—even snakes, etc. 'Doc' always had time for a child with troubles. Even neighborhood mothers, during depression days when money was scarce, would bring sick children to Daddy to see if they were sick enough to warrant the expense of a doctor's visit.

He also used to pile all us kids in the car and take us to the park or the 'Ag Farm' (University of Nebraska Agricultural College.) When I was in high school he used to chauffeur us to the out-of-town football and basketball games. He was really what you could call a 'perfect father.'

Even though his childhood was hard, Louis Vallieres Skidmore went on to have a happy and fulfilling life. And I for one, am thankful for the orphan train and for the Skidmores, who gave my dad a home!

LESTER STUDER

(Interviewed by Michael Patrick, September 1, 1986, and July 14, 1987.)

I was born Lester Mattice on August 10, 1913. My father died before I was born, leaving Mom with two boys and two girls. She finally placed the two boys with the Children's Aid Society of New York March 11, 1915.

Only fourteen days later, Lester and his brother Robert were sent on an orphan train to Fall City, Nebraska. On the day the train arrived, March 27, 1915, L. L. Studer and his wife Agnes Belle were at the station. Their only child had died the year before, and thinking that they would never have another, they had decided to take an orphan into their home. The one they chose that day was two-year-old Lester.

It was not long after that Lester acquired a foster brother. Contrary to their expectations, the Studers did have another child, a son, and eventually two more. The fact that they then had three children of their own did not change their attitude toward Lester. "In the twenty years I lived under their roof, and even after I was married, I never saw any difference in their treatment of me as opposed to their natural children."

Lester's brother Robert, who had come on the same train, was taken by a family named Rule. "Bob and I knew of each other's existence," Lester says, "and for a while we lived as next door neighbors without knowing we were brothers."

Lester's foster father worked for the railroad and Lester thoroughly enjoyed growing up as a roving railroader's son. The family moved frequently. At various times they lived in Osawatomie, Kansas, in Kansas City, and in other towns along the Missouri-Pacific line. They spent part of World War II in Mexico City, where the elder Studer was employed by the U. S. Railway Mission, and finally settled in Sedalia, Missouri.

It was while they were in Mexico that the Children's Aid Society got in touch with the Studer family. They had had a request from Lester's older sisters, Blanche and Bertha, to locate their brothers. The two girls had remained with their mother, raised by her and an aunt. In 1944 Blanche had joined the army and was stationed in New York City. When the Studers received the message, Lester says,

Pop Studer offered to pay my expenses to go back to New York to see my mother and sister. I had no desire to go. I felt that it would be disloyal to the Studers. I also felt that I would have nothing to say to my mother. It would be just like a woman walking down the street that I didn't know telling me that she was my mother when Mom Studer had been my real mother all these years.

He did, however, write to his sisters and his mother wrote to him. After that, communication stopped until 1980.

Meanwhile, Lester grew up to follow in his foster father's footsteps and become a railroad man. He became a pattern maker for the Missouri-Pacific Railroad, living in Sedalia, where he married and raised a family of his own.

Lester grew up thinking that he had been adopted, and after the death of his foster parents he found his adoption papers. Although the papers had been signed both by the Studers and the Children's Aid Society and were notarized, they had never been filed with the probate court. Nevertheless, Lester had been named executor of the Studers' will, and he and the three natural sons received equal shares of the inheritance.

In 1980, after the silence of several years, Lester heard from his sisters again.

At this time I started to make plans to see them. To me, it just didn't seem right to do this with Mom and Pop Studer still living. I was more comfortable about it now. In May of 1981 I called Blanche and told her we would be in Cobbleskill, New York, in a couple of weeks. My wife and I spent two very enjoyable days learning about my sisters.

Lester says that if his sister hadn't looked him up, he might not have planned the reunion. "But now I'm glad we did. I'm real glad." When they met in Cobbleskill there were a few awkward moments, he says. But then they began telling family stories. Lois, his wife, adds, "There weren't many tears. It wasn't that kind of thing. It was more an overwhelming curiosity than anything else."

During their reunion Lester heard for the first time of a great-grandfather who had survived the Civil War. He became the center of family gatherings, because the children could peer through a shell hole in the palm of his hand. He also learned that his natural mother had lived to be eighty-nine. After giving custody of Lester and Robert to the Children's Aid Society, she had married again and had other children. The sisters had never entirely forgiven their mother for having given up their brothers.

By the time they met, Robert had been dead for many

years. Blanche died in 1986. Bertha still lives in New York.

Lester, who was born a Mattice, became so much a part of his foster family that he finds it hard to think of himself as anyone other than a Studer. He is widely known by his nickname Stub, a derivative of Studer. As for his wife, she feels that through her marriage to him the orphan trains are as much a part of her life as of his. And in a poem she has written, she asks many of the questions for which few of the orphans have ever had answers.

ORPHAN TRAIN

Orphan Train, Mercy Train,
What were they really?
Was what these children left behind
better or worse—
than what this train
speeding across the plain—
would enable them to find?

Some left poverty;
Some left death;
Some left a parent that was bereft.
Some left the city streets
where clothing and food
came from the garbage cans,
and all that was good
had to be fought for.

Some were mere babies.
They ate and slept,
and woke and wept,
not really knowing why.
Then the click of the rails
as their lullabys—
sleep, sweet sleep
gave them peace again.

The train made its way
across the plains,
displaying its human wares.
At village and town,
the fold stood around
and watched as the children stepped down—
and the children watched them also.

Who would be chosen?
Who got back on the train?
Who would have to leave a brother?
Who would have to go on again?

Older children were favored
for their strong arms and backs.
Some got food and a bed that was soft;
Some weren't so lucky and slept in a loft.
These chose not to stay—
and ran away.

Some of the very young
filled an aching void
in a mother's heart.
They were accepted
right from the start,
and of this family
became a very real part.

Now seventy years have passed;
survivors are getting together.
They share stories and talk at last
about the good and the bad;
and they wonder whether
being on an orphan train
made their lives so bad,
or just more interesting to others.

PAT THIESSEN

(From the Red Wing Eagle, *September 14, 1985; a story
of the Minnesota orphan train reunion.)*

. . .On a cold November day in 1918, [the child who
became Mrs. Pat Thiessen] arrived [in Red Wing, Min-
nesota] dressed in a delicate white baby dress and petticoat and a hand made cotton coat.

'My mother said I caught a terrible cold dressed like
that in Minnesota weather,' she recounted. Many of the
orphan children became indentured servants and worked
hard for the Midwest family who took them in. 'Not I,'
said Mrs. Thiessen. 'The four older children were grown
and I was the new baby. They always treated me that
way!' Her parents were open about the fact that she was
adopted. 'My mother enjoyed telling people about how I
came to them,' she said, 'and sometimes she added a
little here and there.'

The child had come to Minnesota on a mercy train. She
was taken into the home of a French-Canadian farming
couple, Harmidan and Alphonsine Palnaude, and raised by
them. Only when she was twelve years old did she learn that

her real mother was an Irish woman, who had borne her daughter at the age of twenty. Thirty-eight years later, Mrs. Thiessen received her birth certificate and discovered that her father's name was Finnegan. "I wasn't surprised," she said. "I always felt Irish inside."

Like so many orphan children, she could find out little more about her background. It remained a mystery.

THE WILDE CHILDREN

(Arthur, Elizabeth and Frank)

(From Elizabeth Wilde Daniels, interviewed by Michael Patrick, January 28, 1989; and Mrs. Huberta Lieullan Monger of Kearney, Missouri, undated letter to Evelyn Trickel.)

In 1918 a mercy train left New York with a cargo of twenty orphans. The first stop was a town in Texas, where a pair of twins were left with relatives. The train then made its way north to Missouri, depositing some of the children in Dade County in a community called Pennsboro (which today has a population of twenty-five). There were yet other stops to be made, and Huberta Monger, who lived in Pennsboro as a child, remembers her father's remark: "Oh, there were so many more on the train when it left. . ."

The three Wilde children, passengers on that train, were all placed in the same locality, but in different homes. It would be almost ten years before they found that they had lived near each other all that time. Through subsequent years they kept in touch.

Frank—"so cute and very young at the time"—was the first of the three to be chosen. He went to live with Albert and Kate Lucas. His brother Arthur, who was about twelve and "looked like good help on the farm," was taken by Bailey and Maggie Morris, but only temporarily. As the story goes, the Morris' friends, Will and Rachel Olinger, had only one child, a daughter about twenty. Bailey Morris, figuring that the Olingers needed a son, asked if they would like to take Arthur. They would and they did. "I must say," Mrs. Monger writes in her letter, "a biological son could not look more like his Mother, Rachel Olinger, tall and 'wiry.'"

In 1942 or thereabouts, when Arthur was a grown man, he paid for his own adoption. By that time he was married to Huberta Monger's aunt, and at the adoption ceremony "had a beautiful daughter in his arms." Recalling him fondly, Mrs. Monger writes:

> Uncle Arthur did so well in life, as electrician, and has always helped others—So now Uncle Arthur [Wilde] Olinger is an elderly man, who has added so many wonderful, lovely memories to all of our family. Needless to say, a favorite uncle!

Shortly after Mrs. Monger's letter, Arthur died at his home in San Bernardino, California. Frank, who also had moved to California, is still living in nearby Apple Valley.

Their sister Elizabeth did not fare as well at first as the two boys. In Pennsboro she was moved from family to family seven or eight times, as she remembers, before finding a permanent home with a couple by the name of Tindall. The Tindalls, then in their fifties, had lost their own two children. In January 1922 they had taken a girl named Anna Dulio from another orphan train. In April of that year they took Elizabeth, as well. As it happened, the two girls had known each other in the orphanage in New York. They became as close as natural sisters and lived together with the Tindalls until their marriages—Anna at twenty-six and Elizabeth at twenty-five.

In later years, when their parents were no longer able to look after themselves, the two girls took care of them. "When you've been moved from pillar to post," Elizabeth said, "and at last you find someone who's interested in you, you appreciate them and the home they've given you."

After their parents were gone, Anna and Elizabeth continued to live in the Pennsboro area. Then in 1987 Anna died, and Elizabeth "felt the world had come to an end." She had felt closer to her foster sister than to any other person in her life.

Although the Wildes supposedly had nine or ten siblings, the three who came to Missouri together never heard anything further about the others. Elizabeth Wilde Tindall, who became Mrs. Lyle Daniels, continues to live with her husband in the area where she grew up. The parents of six children, they now have seventeen grandchildren and one great grandchild.

DAVID EDWARD ZIMMERMAN

(From Rosemary Keys, letter to Evelyn Sheets, November 17, 1985.)

The folks in Higginsville, Missouri, called him Smiley. He arrived in Higginsville in 1894, on the same mercy train as Matilda Frank and Cecilia Sheesham. Over the next several years David Zimmerman lived in four different homes: first with Andrew Bonloski, later with Andrew's parents, and for a time with Mrs. Ottilia Wozniak, all of whom lived in or near Higginsville. He was then moved to Kansas City, where he stayed for a while in the home of Joe Schall.

Although we know relatively few of the details of David's life, we know from the story of Matilda Frank (known as Rose Ellen Rogers) that her life was intertwined with his. Both of them passengers on the same train, playmates in grade school, and sweethearts in high school, they were twice engaged to be married and the engagement twice broken. David never married.

Though he left Higginsville for a time, he returned later on. He was a member of the Knights of Columbus and was known for his mission work and for coaching the church softball team. Smiley, as he was known, was killed in 1952 when the car he was driving collided with a truck a mile north of town.

And One Surviving Foster Parent:

MRS. SADIE DICKMAN URTON

(Interviewed by Michael Patrick and Evelyn Trickel.)

One day in 1987, in the sweltering heat of a Missouri summer, I arrived in Trenton, Missouri, where I was met by Evelyn Trickel. Together we drove to the Sunnyview Retirement Home for an interview with a very special lady. Mrs. Sadie Dickman Urton was the foster mother of a child who came on an orphan train, and was the only one we knew of

Sadie Dickman Urton with her first husband, Fred, ca. 1926. *(Courtesy Sadie Urton.)*

who was still living. Her one hundredth birthday was only a month away.

From one of so many years we expected little in the way of information, and we called at the home thinking only to meet her, pay our respects, and go. Little did we realize that we were coming into the presence of a lively lady who only a few days before had won the contest as Queen of the Retirement Home and had started wearing make-up for the first time in her life! To our delight, here was a woman who recalled the past with clarity and humor.

On a day in spring—April 8, 1929, to be exact—Sadie,

who was then Sadie Dickman, and her husband Fred went down to the Trenton depot to see the orphan train come in. Although they had no children of their own at that time, they had never discussed taking a train child. When this particular train came in, there were only four boys left, accompanied by Mr. J. W. Swan, who took them to the Plaza Hotel. Two of the boys were brothers, Martin and Billy Frank. Martin was taken by the Ray Davis family and eleven-year-old Billy went home with Sadie and Fred. Why did she choose Billy? "That's the $64,000 question," Mrs. Urton said. "I just liked his personality." (In the news story, p. 62, Billy Frank is identified as William French, age 13; no mention is made of his brother. Reporting of a small-town weekly is probably responsible for the discrepancy.)

The boy's only memory of his natural mother was that she took his baby sister and a suitcase and left home. Abandoned by his wife, unable to take care of his sons, their father placed them in an orphanage.

Though Billy was small, he was a good worker. One day while helping Fred and Sadie put up hay, Billy pleaded with Fred to let him stack some bales. "You're giving her all the business!"

While Mrs. Urton admits to being "sort of strict" with Billy, she was indulgent too. He loved to ride horses. But since the Dickmans could not always afford a horse, sometimes, when Fred went off to town, Sadie allowed the boy to ride the milk cow.

They worked hard on the farm, but the family had many good times together. Then at seventeen, Billy "was at the age when he knew it all and didn't know anything." As Sadie recalls, he minded her husband but not her. It was not long before a woman from the Children's Aid Society—Mrs. Urton believes it was probably Anne Hill—took Billy to St. Louis to study mechanics at the Rankin School.

After finishing school in 1935 Billy joined the army at Jefferson Barracks. His twenty-year career took him around the world. In World War II he received a battlefield commission in New Guinea, and after the war served in Germany and Iran. Returning, he worked as a civil servant in the gold vaults at Fort Knox. He was married and became the father of three girls and two boys. From them came twelve grand-

Billy Frank, age eleven, soon after his placement with the Dickmans. *(Courtesy Sadie Urton.)*

children. Billy retired in 1971 and died on October 7, 1977. The official cause of death was leukemia. But according to his foster mother, ". . .he died of cigarette smoking. . .If he'd listened to me and not smoked, he'd be living yet."

But in many ways, Billy had listened to her, learning the importance of the family and hard work. A devout man, he always said that his religion came from his foster parents. Throughout his life he kept in touch with them.

Billy's widow, the grandchildren and great-grandchildren still come to visit Sadie Urton. On the day we met her she was looking forward to her birthday on August 21, when the family would come from Kentucky for the party. She graciously invited us to come back and help celebrate.

Toward the end of our conversation, we asked permission to take photographs of her. Mrs. Urton answered with a smile, "Is your camera insured?"

By the time we had talked a while longer, more than two hours had passed and we thought it was time for us to leave. "We don't want to wear you out," I said.

"You won't," she said. And I don't think we did.

We learned a great deal that day.

At this writing Mrs. Urton is still very much alive and approaching one hundred and three.

Bibliography

Abbott, Edith. *Immigration: Select Documents and Case Records.* New York: Ayers Company, 1969.

Beard, Lois Roper. *The History of Laclede County.* Tulsa, Oklahoma: The Heritage Publishing Co., 1979.

Brace, Charles Loring. *The Dangerous Classes of New York and Twenty Years Work Among Them.* Montclair, New Jersey: reprint, Patterson Smith, 1967.

Brace, Emma, ed. *The Life of Charles Loring Brace.* New York: Ayers Company. 1976.

Carlisle, Robert, ed. *Account of Bellevue Hospital.* New York: reprint, Society of Alumni of Bellevue Hospital, 1986.

Daggett, Mabel Potter. "The Child Without a Home." *Delineator* (October 1907), 505-510.

DeWan, George. "When Orphans Went West for a Home." *Newsday* (June 22, 1983, Part II), 4-5.

Fry, Annette Riley. "The Children's Migration." *American Heritage* (December 1974), 4-10.

Hansen, Marcas Lee. *The Atlantic Migration 1607-1860: A History of the Continuing Settlement of the United States.* New York: Harper & Row, 1962.

Holloran, Peter. *Boston's Wayward Children: Social Services for Homeless Children, 1830-1930.* Cranbury, New Jersey: Fairleigh Dickinson University Press, 1989.

Homan, Eve. "Passage of Promise." *CGA World* (November/December 1984), 28-30.

Israels II, Joseph. "Not Wanted." *Saturday Evening Post* (December 18, 1948), 90-95.

Jackson, Donald Dale. "It Took Trains to Put Street Kids on the Right Track Out of the Slums." *Smithsonian Magazine* (August 1986), 95-103.

Kadushin, Alfred. *Child Welfare Services.* New York: The Macmillan Company. n.d.

King, Charles. "Homelessness in America." *The Humanist* (May/June 1989), 7-15.

Kozol, Jonathan. *Rachel and Her Children: Homeless Families in America.* New York: Crown Publishers, 1988.

Langsam, Miriam Z. *Children West: A History of the Placing-Out System of the New York Children's Aid Society 1853-*

1890. Madison: State Historical Society of Wisconsin, 1964.

Lemonine, Rachel. "Sentimental Journey: Children of the Orphan Trains." *Louisiana Life* (May-June 1985), 58-62.

Magnuson, James, and Dorothea Petrie. *Orphan Train: A Novel.* New York: Dover, 1978.

Patrick, Michael, Evelyn Sheets, and Evelyn Trickel, creative consultants. "End of the Line." Video. St. Louis: Heritage Account, Inc., 1989.

Vogt, Martha Nelson, and Christina Vogt. *Searching for Home: Three Families from the Orphan Trains, a True Story.* Grand Rapids, Michigan: Triumph Press, 1985.

Von Hartz, John. *New York Street Kids.* New York: Dover, 1978.

Wheeler, Leslie. "The Orphan Trains." *American History Illustrated* (December 1983), 10-23.

Wiens, Henrietta. "I was on the Orphan Train." *The Plain Truth.* (April 1984), 31-32, 43.

Index